The Cyber Security Handbook

Prepare for, respond to and recover from cyber attacks with the IT Governance Cyber Resilience Framework (CRF)

The Cyber Security Handbook

Prepare for, respond to and recover from cyber attacks with the IT Governance Cyber Resilience Framework (CRF)

ALAN CALDER

IT Governance Publishing

IT Governance Publishing Ltd
Unit 3, Clive Court
Bartholomew's Walk
Cambridgeshire Business Park
Ely, Cambridgeshire
CB7 4EA
United Kingdom
www.itgovernancepublishing.co.uk

First edition published in the United Kingdom in 2020 by IT Governance Publishing

ISBN 978-1-78778-407-9

ABOUT THE AUTHOR

Alan Calder founded IT Governance Limited in 2002 and began working full time for the company in 2007. He is now Group CEO of GRC International Group plc, the AIM-listed company that owns IT Governance Ltd. Prior to this, Alan had a number of roles including CEO of Business Link London City Partners from 1995 to 1998 (a government agency focused on helping growing businesses to develop), CEO of Focus Central London from 1998 to 2001 (a training and enterprise council), CEO of Wide Learning from 2001 to 2003 (a supplier of e-learning) and the Outsourced Training Company (2005). Alan was also chairman of CEME (a public private sector skills partnership) from 2006 to 2011.

Alan is an acknowledged international cyber security guru and a leading author on information security and IT governance issues. He has been involved in the development of a wide range of information security management training courses that have been accredited by the International Board for IT Governance Qualifications (IBITGQ). Alan has consulted for clients in the UK and abroad, and is a regular media commentator and speaker.

CONTENTS

Part 1: Introduction

CHAPTER 1: THE THREAT LANDSCAPE

We live in a world where technology and vast quantities of data play a considerable role in everyday life, personal and professional. For the foreseeable future (and perhaps beyond), their growth and prominence are showing no signs of slowing down, even if the technology in question will likely change in ways perhaps unimaginable today. Naturally, all this innovation brings huge opportunities and benefits to companies and individuals alike. However, these come at more than just a financial cost.

In the world as we know it, you can be attacked both physically and virtually. For today's organisations, which rely so heavily on technology – particularly the Internet – to do business, the latter is the far more threatening of the two. The cyber threat landscape is complex and constantly changing. For every vulnerability fixed, another pops up, ripe for exploitation. Worse, when a vulnerability is identified, a tool that can exploit it is often developed and used within hours – faster than the time it normally takes for the vendor to release a patch, and certainly quicker than the time many organisations take to install that patch.

The fact that technology is involved gives attackers a huge advantage over the defenders – not only can they attack anyone, anywhere, from the comfort of their home, they often have automated tools to identify their victims – and their vulnerabilities – for them. Moreover, from an attacker's perspective, there is often a very good risk-to-reward ratio: for the victim, it can be hard enough to detect that the attack happened at all, never mind trace who was behind it. It is the very nature of the digital information that we are trying to protect that is easy to copy. In fact, stealing the information does not require removing it from its original location at all, meaning that the owner of that information may never realise that the theft happened.

Unfortunately for us, committing crimes over the Internet can also be very lucrative. Physical pickpocketing may earn a thief cash and credit cards (that will likely be blocked very quickly, and can probably only be used up to the contactless limit per transaction anyway), but digitally targeting someone gives them a chance to steal that person's identity and get credit cards issued in the victim's name. Upscale that, and a criminal might think about targeting businesses that hold databases with thousands or even millions of credit card details and personal information about their owners. Whether they then directly use that information for themselves or sell it on the dark web (where you can buy virtually anything, from drugs and organs to hacking software and stolen credentials), the profits are certainly far greater than those of a physical crime conducted in the same timescale and with the same manpower.

Because virtually every organisation holds valuable information, often in huge quantities (even if you are a small business), everyone is a target. More often than not, organisations cannot do business if they lose access to that information – making it one of their most important assets. At the same time, the fact that criminals can extract significant value from this information means that it is an asset to them too. There is good reason to refer to them as information 'assets' – by definition, someone else wants to get hold of them. Many a time, that 'someone' is a business partner who will go through the proper channels – but not everyone will take the legal route.

It should therefore not come as a surprise that 46% of UK businesses alone experienced at least one cyber attack or breach during 2019, which increased to as much as 75% for large businesses.[1] Such attacks might range from simple phishing emails to complex, detailed operations masterminded by criminal gangs – although the trend over the past five years, according to the UK government's 2020 Cyber Security Breaches Survey, is that cyber attacks are evolving and becoming more frequent[2] – but even the simplest attack, if executed successfully, can wreak havoc if you are not prepared. Clearly, it is in your organisation's best interests to protect itself. Although this might cost, it will certainly prove far cheaper than experiencing a breach and having to deal with the operational, financial and reputational damage that follows.

Yet, given the frequency of data breaches and cyber attacks in the press, many of them large-scale, you could be forgiven for thinking that it is impossible to defend your organisation against the predations of cyber attackers – after all, if massive multinationals cannot stay secure, what hope is there for small businesses?

The answer is: more than you think. Cyber security does not have to cost vast amounts of money or take years to implement, particularly if you take a strategic approach and aim for the lower-hanging fruit first. And it is a worthwhile investment: no matter the size of your organisation,

---

[1] UK Department for Digital, Culture, Media & Sport, "Cyber Security Breaches Survey 2020", March 2020, *https://www.gov.uk/government/publications/cyber-security-breaches-survey-2020/cyber-security-breaches-survey-2020*.

[2] Ibid.

improving cyber security helps protect your data and that of your clients, improving business relations and opening up new business opportunities.

CHAPTER 2: INFORMATION AND CYBER SECURITY

The terms 'information security' and 'cyber security' are often used interchangeably, when in fact they refer to different (albeit related) things.

To start with the similarities, both information and cyber security are concerned with security on three fronts:

1. **Confidentiality:**
   Information assets and systems should only be accessible to those who need access.
2. **Integrity:**
   Information assets and systems should be protected from unauthorised modification, destruction and loss.
3. **Availability:**
   Information assets and systems should be accessible to authorised persons as and when necessary.

Considering all three aspects of security (also referred to as 'CIA') means that you will not make the common mistake of only taking confidentiality into account. Clearly, restricting information on a need-to-know basis is a critical element of security, but that information is only useful if you know it is correct and you are able to access it when you need it.

There are, however, some important distinctions to draw between information and cyber security. The former considers *all* information held by an organisation, irrespective of whether that information is electronic or in hard copy format, whereas cyber security is a subset of information security, focusing specifically on protecting electronic information.

Even though cyber security may seem like the more obvious route for organisations to take, considering how our world is becoming increasingly digitalised, there will always be an element of physical security to consider, if only because you need to protect your hardware to be able to access your digital information. On top of the matter of availability, firewalls and anti-malware software cannot completely protect your devices if someone can just look over your shoulder at what you are doing or take the device altogether.

Part 3 of this book delves into the sort of measures you can take to protect your organisation from these risks.

CHAPTER 3: CYBER RESILIENCE

Unfortunately, even the most secure organisation can still fall victim to a cyber attack. To a large extent, it is simply a case of having the odds stacked against you: although you need to protect *all* your assets from *all* types of threat, an attacker requires only *one* weakness to get into your systems. On top of that, any security measure you put in place is only designed to stop a handful of threats – at most. That means that it is likely to be inherently ineffective against other kinds of threat.

It is important both to recognise these challenges and to not view them as insurmountable.

To understand why the former is so important, you only have to look at the past. History teaches us that if you assume that something cannot possibly go wrong, you may find it difficult, if not impossible, to remedy the situation if it goes wrong anyway. The Germans in World War II deemed the Enigma machine to be uncrackable, so never even considered the possibility that the British were intercepting and decrypting their messages. The RMS *Titanic* was deemed unsinkable, so only had 20 lifeboats with capacity for just over 1,000 people, when the ship itself had capacity for more than 3,000 individuals.

On the other hand, acknowledging that your security system may fail despite your best efforts enables you to pre-emptively consider how something might go wrong and what you can do to limit the damage in such a situation. In other words, thinking *resiliently* will enable you to recover from attack – even if rare, when one happens, the consequences can be crippling if you have not planned how you will respond.

Taking a defence-in-depth approach, where you have multiple layers of defence, each defending against a specific – and different – type of threat (this concept is discussed further in 12.12.8), is an excellent place to start. It is also vital that you do not limit your defences to preventive measures (see chapter 12), but also put detective measures (see chapter 13) in place – so you know when your preventive measures have failed – as well as responsive measures (see chapter 14), so you can move swiftly to contain the damage.

CHAPTER 4: REGULATORY AND CONTRACTUAL REQUIREMENTS

If the fact that your organisation needs to wade through a complex cyber threat landscape in order to compete in today's digital world is in itself not a strong enough case to invest in cyber security and resilience, the added pressure from a global regulatory system that is beginning to catch up might be.

4.1 International data privacy laws

The introduction of the EU General Data Protection Regulation (GDPR) in 2016 – which was enforced two years later – marked a major milestone for data protection and privacy laws across the world. Most of us remember the flood of 'we need your consent' emails that arrived in our inboxes in the days leading up to and after the GDPR took effect,[3] but those emails were only the tip of the iceberg.

The GDPR places a wide range of security and privacy obligations on organisations that process the data of EU residents and is supported by a regime of significant financial penalties (up to the greater of 4% of annual turnover or €20 million (about £18 million or $23 million)). The GDPR also requires organisations based outside of the

---

[3] As an aside, not all of those emails were necessary. Consent is only one of six lawful bases for processing – if you need to contact someone to provide a service in order to fulfil a contract, for instance, you can rely on contractual necessity. As another example, if you already have a commercial relationship with someone, you can often rely on legitimate interests to send them relevant marketing material.

EU that process personal data on EU residents to appoint an EU representative, extending the reach of those obligations and penalties far beyond the EU's physical borders. The Regulation is further enforced on an international level by prohibiting EU organisations from transferring data outside the EEA unless the recipient organisation in a 'third country' can guarantee that the GDPR's standard for data security will be met.

However, the GDPR is not the only data privacy law to have emerged in recent years. California and Brazil have respectively seen the California Privacy Rights Act (CPRA) and Lei Geral de Proteção de Dados Pessaoais (General Data Privacy Law) introduced, and further regulatory action on an international level is expected in the coming years.

4.2 Cyber security requirements for critical infrastructure

The increasing regulatory focus on data protection, privacy and continuity of key services inevitably leads to an increasing focus on cyber security, as so much of the information held by organisations is in electronic formats. Many organisations, including the majority of essential services, also rely on an electronic infrastructure.

In view of that reliance, laws such as the EU Directive on security of network and information systems (NIS Directive) have also been introduced in recent years. This directive places specific cyber security and incident response obligations on digital service providers, including Cloud service providers and operators of essential services (OES), such as power and water, with a view to mitigating the disruption that could occur as the result of a major cyber security incident.

For these types of critical providers, a successful cyber attack can easily have an impact in the physical world – think, for example, about the impact WannaCry had on the UK's National Health Service, where thousands of appointments had to be cancelled.[4] Because the health sector is such a vital one to keep going whatever the circumstances, healthcare organisations may well face additional cyber security requirements, such as the Data Security and Protection (DSP) Toolkit for the UK, and the Health Insurance Portability and Accountability Act (HIPAA) for the US.

4.3 Contractual requirements

It is not just laws that mandate effective cyber security. Cyber security obligations in contracts are also becoming increasingly common, as organisations better recognise the risks posed by information-sharing between suppliers and partners (third-party threats are discussed in more detail in chapter 10).

If your organisation takes card payments, for example, banks will expect you to adhere to the requirements of the Payment Card Industry Data Security Standard (PCI DSS). As another example, many government contracts mandate a minimum level of cyber security to enter the tendering process, and often ask for proof in the form of certification to a recognised standard. Big, long-term contracts now commonly also ask for a minimum level of security, and for it to be proven in a supplier audit or through some form of externally verified

---

[4] BBC News, "NHS 'could have prevented' WannaCry ransomware attack", October 2017, *https://www.bbc.co.uk/news/technology-41753022*.

certification. Organisations bound by these obligations are often also required to ensure comparable security throughout their supply chains.

CHAPTER 5: IMPLEMENTING CYBER SECURITY

Although chapter 1 mentioned that cyber security need not be expensive, and that your implementation does not need to take a long time, it can still be difficult to know where to start.

In truth, there are many different and valid ways of implementing cyber security. The correct one for your organisation depends on your goals and requirements, so a good place to start is by clearly defining what they are. Our eight-step approach to implementing cyber security, laid out in part 4 of this book, will discuss in more detail how you might do this. For now, think about basic questions such as:

- How do you identify threats and vulnerabilities? Is that process consistently applied?
- What are your most important assets, and what level of protection do they need?
- Are there specific regulatory or contractual requirements for cyber security that you must meet?
- What level of security do your customers expect?
- What do your competitors do in terms of security?
- Do you rely on and/or offer services that must meet a minimum level of availability?
- If you suffered a cyber incident or data breach, what would the consequences be?
- How would you know an incident occurred?

At this stage, do not worry about coming up with comprehensive answers – these questions are just intended to help get your juices flowing.

5.1 Making trade-offs

Whatever approach to security you take – even if that is to do nothing at all – there are always trade-offs to make.

Doing nothing might be cheaper and more convenient in the short term, but with the inevitability of sooner or later being attacked, in the long term you may end up with a big bill and significant inconvenience (dealing with regulators and the press, operational impact, etc.). However, putting security measures in place also involves making trade-offs. To name but two examples, some solutions will be cheaper but might only protect you against one type of attack, while others might be more expensive but easier to implement or more convenient to use and maintain.

Budget, privacy, convenience, complexity, resources, time, flexibility, etc. may all need to be considered as you decide what trade-offs to make and what solutions to implement. Ultimately, this process lies at the very heart of security, cyber or otherwise: deciding what sacrifices you are prepared to make (and are necessary) so you can meet your security requirements. More simply put, much like many other decisions in life, it is a process of weighing up the pros and cons. There is no such thing as perfect security, but there are solutions out there that are perfect for meeting your security needs.

5.2 Three security pillars

As you make your security trade-offs, be aware that your measures have to cover the three security 'pillars' – people, processes and technology – if you are to create an effective security system. People often just think about what technology to implement when they invest in cyber security, overlooking that any technical measures need to be implemented and maintained by people, who need to follow defined processes.

The 'people' element is not limited to specialist staff. With the prevalence of the internal threat, any authorised user that has access to your systems can be a risk factor. They are often not maliciously motivated, but could have made a mistake – whether it is something relatively pedestrian, such as losing a USB stick, or something more exceptional, such as falling for a sophisticated phishing attack – that results in a data breach, installs malware, gives the attacker access to their account or any number of other cyber incidents. Chapter 8 has a more detailed discussion on the human threat.

Of course, technology can help mitigate these threats to an extent – for instance, by installing anti-malware software and firewalls. However, much in tune with the earlier trade-off discussion, these solutions are not perfect, even if they can help prevent many common and low-level attacks. You will need some form of staff training and awareness if your employees are to recognise phishing attempts and other indicators of a cyber attack, and respond accordingly, in line with the appropriate policies and procedures.

There are many more examples in which the three pillars clearly interact. Lockable cabinets are not very helpful if people forget to lock them overnight (or worse still, do not put confidential documents in them in the first place). If the person next to the intercom has to regularly buzz colleagues in because people forget their ID card, they may habitually not actually check who they are letting in. Having your password policy enforce complex passwords is not much use if people reuse passwords or write them down, etc.

There is, however, one final point to remember, which is easily overlooked. Where people are involved, security can be both a feeling and a reality, and there are many cases in which only one of them is true. Most people consider flying less secure than driving, for instance, yet the statistics consistently show that aeroplane crashes are far rarer than fatal driving accidents. In a cyber security context, the knowledge that antivirus software has been installed might make you feel safe, and perhaps make you more careless when surfing the web than you otherwise would be. Such dangers should be considered as you select your security measures.

5.3 The IT Governance Cyber Resilience Framework (CRF)

Admittedly, there is a lot to take in when it comes to cyber security. However, you do not need to do all the legwork yourself – for a start, books such as this one can offer a trove of practical tips and guidance. There are also many frameworks available that can offer you an existing and proven structure to work from, reassuring you that you are heading in the right direction. There is a big range to choose from, although in the UK two are particularly common: Cyber Essentials, which has just five basic controls, and ISO 27001, which contains a substantial 114 controls, although you are only expected to implement those relevant to you. Part 5 of this book summarises ten different best-practice frameworks, so you can get an idea of the options available, and which might be suitable for your organisation.

If these types of frameworks, for whatever reason, are not for you, rest assured that this book primarily offers content in line with best practice without referring to any external standard or framework. However, since this book still needs to be structured in an easy-to-follow format, the security controls and implementation steps covered are based on the IT Governance CRF, depicted in part in Table 1.

This framework, first released in February 2019,[5] forms a good base for any cyber security project for a number of reasons:

- It has a comprehensive selection of processes (see the first column in Table 1), reducing the odds of overlooking any areas that require security controls.
- The process selection is extremely flexible – you only implement the measures that you need based on your compliance and business requirements. Because of this, you can treat part 3 of this book (where each CRF process is discussed in detail) in an encyclopaedic way if you want to – reading just the bits you need in an order of your choice (although reading it from beginning to end works just as well). Chapter 11 provides a summary of each process, enabling you to quickly determine which processes you need to look at further.
- The Framework offers further flexibility in its four maturity levels, discussed in more detail in chapter 16.

---

[5] IT Governance, "IT Governance releases its Cyber Resilience Framework to help organisations stay ahead of cyber risks", February 2019, *https://www.itgovernance.co.uk/media/press-releases/it-governance-releases-its-cyber-resilience-framew*.

> This means that, on top of excluding any processes you do not need, you implement the ones you keep only to the level of sophistication that you need.

The CRF also provides a detailed mapping of its processes against four common sets of compliance requirements. Naturally, every organisation must meet different requirements to different degrees, so it is important that you determine exactly what yours are. Chapter 19 discusses how you can go about this.

Table 1: The IT Governance CRF (excludes reference frameworks)

	Compliance requirements				[Mapping to reference frameworks – detail provided in part 5, chapters 26–30]
	GDPR	*PCI DSS*	*NIS Regulations*[6]	*DSP Toolkit*	
Manage and protect					
Asset management	✓	✓	✓	✓	
Information security policies	✓	✓	✓	✓	
Physical and environmental security	✓	✓	✓	✓	
Identity and access control	✓	✓	✓	✓	
Malware protection	✓	✓	✓	✓	
Configuration and patch management	✓	✓	✓	✓	
Encryption	✓	✓	✓		
System security	✓	✓	✓	✓	

[6] The Network and Information Systems Regulations 2018; the UK implementation of the EU NIS Directive. This column only applies to UK operators of essential services (OES).

Network and communications security	✓	✓	✓	✓
Security competence and training	✓	✓	✓	✓
Staff awareness training	✓	✓	✓	✓
Comprehensive risk management programme	✓	✓	✓	
Supply chain risk management	✓	✓	✓	
Identify and detect				
Threat and vulnerability intelligence	✓	✓	✓	✓
Security monitoring	✓	✓	✓	✓
Respond and recover				
Incident response management	✓	✓	✓	✓
ICT continuity management		✓	✓	✓
Business continuity management		✓	✓	
Govern and assure				

Formal information security management programme	✓	✓	✓	✓	
Continual improvement process					
Board-level commitment and involvement		✓	✓	✓	
Governance structure and processes			✓	✓	
Internal audit		✓	✓		
External certification/ validation		✓	✓	✓	

5.4 Structure of the book

This book is divided into six parts:

Part 1: Introduction

The world of cyber security and the approach taken in this book.

Part 2: Threats and vulnerabilities

A discussion of a range of threats organisations face, organised by threat category, to help you understand what you are defending yourself against before you start thinking about your actual defences.

Part 3: The CRF processes

Detailed discussions of each of the 24 CRF processes, explaining a wide range of security areas by process category and offering guidance on how to implement each.

Part 4: Eight steps to implementing cyber security

Our eight-step approach to implementing the cyber security processes you need and maintaining them.

Part 5: Reference frameworks

An explanation of how standards and frameworks work, along with their benefits. It also presents ten framework options, introducing you to some of the best-known standards and giving you an idea of the range available.

Part 6: Conclusion and appendices

Concluding the manual. The appendices include a glossary of all the acronyms and abbreviations used in this book.

Part 2: Threats and vulnerabilities

CHAPTER 6: THE ANATOMY OF THREATS

As we have seen, for all the benefits of the cyber world, it also brings significant risk. Much like any other type of risk, cyber security risk derives from a combination of threats and vulnerabilities – vulnerabilities are exploited by threats to achieve certain goals, such as accessing a secure network or installing malware. This does not mean that cyber security risk is limited to deliberate actions by malicious actors, however – a leaky roof in a server room (vulnerability), for instance, can be 'exploited' by a rainstorm (threat) with potentially catastrophic results. Developing an understanding of what threats you may face and the sort of vulnerabilities you need to look out for are vital preparatory steps to developing effective defences.

Threats and vulnerabilities can take many forms. A database that fails to properly sanitise user inputs, for instance, might be exploited by an attacker using an SQL injection to gain access to sensitive data, while unpatched software might allow an attacker to install malware, with any number of nasty results – wiping files completely or holding them to ransom, to name just two.

Hardware and software are always evolving, and the same is true for vulnerabilities – each innovation brings new security challenges. Even longstanding, trusted software and hardware are not immune. In 2018, major computer chip manufacturers were stunned to discover that their processors had major, hardware-level security flaws (named 'Meltdown' and 'Spectre') since 1995 – processors that are believed to be in almost every modern computer across the globe.[7]

Cyber threat actors come in all shapes and sizes too. Although our first thought may be of the 'nerd' locked in a basement writing code for a prank, the reality is very different. Organised crime gangs, 'hacktivists' pushing a political agenda and even state-supported actors all represent potential threats, irrespective of the size of your organisation. One of the reasons every organisation is a target is that many attacks are opportunistic, targeting vulnerabilities rather than companies.

A particularly pervasive threat actor is something you cannot survive without: your employees. Even discounting employees who are actively looking to harm their organisation in some way (often because they are unhappy), many cyber security incidents are caused inadvertently, through human error, because an employee did not understand the risks or because they simply made a mistake. According to the 2020 Insider Threat Report, 70% of responding organisations experienced at least one insider attack in 2019.[8]

This part of the book covers a range of threats, organised by threat type. The list is nowhere near exhaustive (in any case,

---

[7] Samuel Gibbs, "Meltdown and Spectre: 'worst ever' CPU bugs affect virtually all computers", *The Guardian*, January 2018, *https://www.theguardian.com/technology/2018/jan/04/meltdown-spectre-worst-cpu-bugs-ever-found-affect-computers-intel-processors-security-flaw*.

[8] Cybersecurity Insiders, "2020 Insider Threat Report", November 2019, *https://www.cybersecurity-insiders.com/portfolio/2020-insider-threat-report/*.

since new threats and vulnerabilities are discovered all the time, it would be impossible to do so in this type of publication), but it should give some insight into the most common threat types, and a sense of their diversity. Part 3 of this book talks in depth about how to address these threats, and how to generally identify and mitigate the risks you may face.

CHAPTER 7: TECHNICAL THREATS

Most of the time, when people think about cyber security, they think of technical threats first. The media regularly features stories of vast data breaches that are eventually traced to some hardware or software vulnerability, both obscure and otherwise. In 2011–2020, malware increased by a staggering 1,634%.[9] In less than two months, one million phishing emails were reported to the UK's National Cyber Security Centre (NCSC) alone.[10]

Although the NCSC successfully blocked or took down thousands of malicious websites, undoubtedly many more new ones have since appeared in their place. Unfortunately, attackers often have the upper hand, having to find and successfully exploit just one vulnerability when defenders need to protect themselves against every type of attack. The expression that your security is only as strong as your weakest link is very apt here.

7.1 The attackers

Before you can protect yourself, you need to understand who is attacking you and what their weapons are. At the most basic level, criminal hackers concern themselves with finding and exploiting flaws and vulnerabilities in hardware

---

[9] AV-TEST, "Malware", accessed July 2020, *https://www.av-test.org/en/statistics/malware/*.

[10] NCSC, "Thanks a million: British public help reach major milestone in fight against scammers", June 2020, *https://www.ncsc.gov.uk/news/british-public-help-reach-milestone-against-scammers*.

and software. There is no shortage of flaws to find, either – no piece of software or hardware is truly immune, and new vulnerabilities are identified every single day. Zero-day vulnerabilities (a vulnerability that the vendor is not yet aware of) are a favourite target of criminal hackers, as attacks are more likely to be successful.

Criminal hackers are a disparate group encompassing everything from the stereotypical basement-dwelling nerd to state-supported 'hacker teams' with extensive resources. To better classify the threat posed by each type of criminal hacker, they are usually categorised as follows.

7.1.1 Script kiddie

This term refers to low-skilled, often young hackers who use prebuilt tools to carry out low-sophistication attacks, often without any real understanding of the underlying principles. Although this does not make them any less threatening – their tools are built by skilled hackers who know exactly what they are doing, after all – it does mean that the vulnerabilities they exploit are usually common ones for which fixes are likely already available, and against which basic cyber security measures such as regular patching (see 12.6.2) often offer protection.

A notable proportion of cyber crime occurs in exactly this way – inexperienced malicious actors purchasing simple tools or botnets to carry out low-level attacks that, despite their simplicity, still present a tenable threat to the organisation, particularly if you use out-of-date hardware or software, with potentially serious consequences. Many script kiddies have little or no appreciation of the wider effects of their attacks or the principles that underpin them, in part because it is so easy to buy hacking tools and malware kits online. They have little concept of the real effect or cost of their attacks and will often claim that the attack was only done 'for the lols'.

7.1.2 Black hats

Skilled criminal hackers who identify new vulnerabilities and develop the tools used to exploit them are known as 'black hats'. Financial motivation is common – many black hats sell the hacking tools they develop on the dark web, though they may also carry out attacks themselves in the hope of extorting payment (for example, via ransomware) or selling stolen information to other criminals.

Unlike script kiddies, black hats know exactly what they are doing and usually have a clear idea of what they want to achieve from a given attack. As a result, they are some of the most effective and feared attackers.

7.1.3 Hacktivists

A 'hacktivist' is more a classification of motivation than of skill or ability. Hacktivists carry out attacks to promote an agenda, though the ideology behind the agenda is often ill-defined and may vary over time. Hacktivist attacks are difficult to predict, not only because of the disparate nature of the groups themselves, but also because of the wide range of potential targets. Notorious hacktivist group 'Anonymous', for example, has conducted attacks on the

Church of Scientology, Sony Online Entertainment, the Islamic State and Donald Trump, to name but a few.[11]

7.1.4 State actors and cyber warfare

Cyber warfare may seem like something out of a science fiction novel, but cyber attacks carried out by nation state actors are increasingly common. In July 2019, Microsoft reported that it had notified almost 10,000 customers (84% of which were enterprise accounts) that they had been "targeted or compromised by nation state attacks" over the course of the previous year.[12]

State-sponsored attackers often have access to extensive funding and equipment, and may operate with actual or tacit legal immunity in their country, making them very difficult (but not impossible) to bring to justice. Nation state attacks also tend to be highly targeted and focused on achieving specific goals, such as disrupting critical infrastructure or exfiltrating intellectual property. The 2010 Stuxnet attack on Iranian nuclear facilities is an infamous example of cyber warfare in action. This targeted the programmable logic controllers that managed the centrifuges, changing spinning

---

[11] Brian Feldman, "An Incomplete List of Every Person, Place, and Institution Upon Which Anonymous Has 'Declared War'", *Intelligencer*, March 2016, *http://nymag.com/intelligencer/2016/03/everything-upon-which-anonymous-has-declared-war.html*.

[12] Tom Burt, "New cyberthreats require new ways to protect democracy", *Microsoft*, July 2019, *https://blogs.microsoft.com/on-the-issues/2019/07/17/new-cyberthreats-require-new-ways-to-protect-democracy/*.

speeds and causing the centrifuges to disintegrate.[13] More recently, during the race to find a vaccine for Covid-19 in 2020, both the Chinese[14] and Russian[15] governments were accused of sponsoring criminal hackers to attempt to steal British, American and Canadian coronavirus research.

7.1.5 Ethical hacking

Not every hacker is a cyber criminal. Ethical hackers use the same tools and techniques as criminal hackers to search for vulnerabilities, but instead of exploiting them, they inform the system operator so that the vulnerabilities can be fixed. This approach, known as 'penetration testing', helps organisations identify and resolve vulnerabilities before they fall victim to an attack.

Penetration testing is discussed in more detail in 13.1.3.

7.2 Malware

Malware has existed in one form or another since computers became commonplace. Self-replicating software was first conceived in the 1940s, and one of the first viruses, known as the 'Creeper', was created in the early 1970s, infecting US

---

[13] David Kushner, "The Real Story of Stuxnet", *IEEE Spectrum*, February 2013, *https://spectrum.ieee.org/telecom/security/the-real-story-of-stuxnet.*

[14] BBC News, "US charges Chinese hackers for wide-ranging activities, including Covid research intrusions", July 2020, *https://edition.cnn.com/2020/07/21/politics/china-hackers-coronavirus/index.html*.

[15] Chris Fox and Leo Kelion, "Coronavirus: Russian spies target Covid-19 vaccine research", *BBC News*, July 2020, *https://www.bbc.co.uk/news/technology-53429506*.

government computers and displaying "I'm the Creeper, catch me if you can" on the screen.

Since then, there has been an explosion of malware. Sites on the dark web offer a vast array of malware programs for sale, and new malware appears daily, taking advantage of the latest vulnerabilities in a never-ending arms race between the malicious actors that craft it and the cyber security professionals who defend against it. 'Malware' as a category encompasses a range of malicious programs, each of which operates differently.

7.2.1 Virus

Viruses are self-replicating programs designed to spread from computer to computer and deliver a payload. Viruses are not standalone programs – they are bits of code that need to be hidden in other programs to function and replicate. When the user runs the 'host' program, the virus infects the system and sets about doing its work.

Once it has infected a system, the virus has two goals: replicate itself as much as possible and deliver the payload, preferably without being spotted. Some of the earliest viruses were called 'boot sector' viruses, as they infected sections of a drive that were read when a computer booted up, making them hard to detect, and were often spread through the sharing of floppy disks (which were common at the time).

Some of the most common viruses of the Internet era are 'macro' viruses – viruses written in the scripting language found in Microsoft Office and embedded into Office files, such as Excel spreadsheets or Word documents. Opening the document allows the virus to infect the system, with potentially catastrophic results. Emails featuring infected

Office documents have been a common attack vector since the early '90s, so much so that 'do not open suspicious attachments' has become a cyber security maxim.

7.2.2 Worms

If the principal characteristic of a virus is that it is a self-replicating program that must be embedded in another program to function, then a worm is a virus with that limitation removed. Worms do not need to be embedded in other programs and can replicate without user interaction, making them especially dangerous.

One of the best-known worms in recent years is Stuxnet, which was briefly discussed in 7.1.4.

7.2.3 Ransomware

Ransomware exploded into the public consciousness with the worldwide WannaCry attack in 2017. Ransomware is a payload, usually transmitted by self-replicating worms or Trojans, that encrypts or otherwise prevents access to the user's files until a ransom is paid (usually in Bitcoin). Some ransomware will take a copy of the user's files and threaten to publish them, but the effect is the same – pay up or lose out.

Before the WannaCry attack, ransomware primarily targeted individual consumers. The 2017 attacks marked the beginning of a shift in focus, with 81% of ransomware attacks in 2018 targeting organisations, not consumers.[16]

7.2.4 Trojan horses

Trojan horses, or just 'Trojans', are a type of malware that pretend to be something else. The name arises from the ancient Greek story about the wooden horse that led to the fall of Troy.

Trojans generally masquerade as legitimate programs to trick you into activating them, though some can spread on their own without user interaction. One of the most common attack vectors is email, as Trojans can be embedded into seemingly innocuous attachments such as spreadsheets or Word files. Once activated, the Trojan sends spoof emails to everyone in the address book, further spreading the infection.

Trojans can carry almost any kind of payload, but keyloggers (which record what keys on a keyboard are struck) and 'backdoors' that give access to sensitive information or systems are common. Trojans that contain keyloggers or other methods of capturing information usually send the information to a master server from time to time; these transmissions can sometimes be the only way of detecting the presence of the Trojan.

---

[16] Symantec, "Internet Security Threat Report (ISTR) Volume 24", February 2019, *https://symantec-enterprise-blogs.security.com/blogs/threat-intelligence/istr-24-cyber-security-threat-landscape*.

7.2.5 Hybrid malware

Hybrid malware is malware that combines different aspects of other malware in order to be more effective.

Most of the malware we encounter today is a hybrid – for example, a worm with a ransomware payload, such as WannaCry. Worms with Trojan or rootkit payloads are responsible for most 'botnets' – connected groups of computers or other Internet-enabled devices that are used to conduct distributed denial-of-service (DDoS) attacks, where a large number of devices communicate with the target simultaneously in order to overload it. Internet of Things (IoT) devices are particularly prone to botnet infections and related threats because they tend to have less effective security at both hardware and software levels (though this is beginning to change as awareness of IoT threats increases).

7.2.6 Living-off-the-land and fileless malware

A relatively recent development in the cyber threat landscape, 'living-off-the-land' attacks involve the use of legitimate system and administrative tools (such as PowerShell or TeamViewer) that are already installed on the target system. These attacks can be difficult to detect, as the malicious activity blends in with other, legitimate administrative use of such tools.

A related concept is 'fileless' malware. Living-off-the-land techniques are sometimes called fileless malware as they only involve existing, legitimate software, and do not require, for example, the user to download an infected file. This is not entirely accurate; instead, fileless malware is better thought of as an attack that does not require or generate additional files that anti-malware software might identify as suspicious. Examples include malware that run and deliver their payload entirely within system memory, scripts embedded into the Windows registry system and some browser-based cryptojacking attacks.

7.3 Technical threat example: TalkTalk data breach

In 2015, TalkTalk was hit by an SQL injection attack that exposed the personal data of more than 150,000 customers, for which the UK's Information Commissioner's Office (ICO) proposed a fine of £400,000 (about $515,000) (later settled under agreement for £320,000 (about $412,000)).

The ICO's report noted multiple cyber security failings alongside the SQL injection vulnerability, including two previous SQL injection attacks on the same web pages that went unnoticed because of a lack of monitoring. To make matters worse, the exposed customer information was stored in an outdated legacy database that lacked a security fix made available by the vendor more than three years earlier (which would have prevented the attack, had it been applied).[17]

An effective secure development process would have prevented this problem from ever occurring. Code injection attacks have been a known, recurring vulnerability for more than 20 years and any effective secure development process would have highlighted this fact. The same is true for the legacy database – an effective process would have highlighted the risks associated with unsupported software,

[17] Alex Hern, "TalkTalk hit with record £400k fine over cyber-attack", *The Guardian*, October 2016, *https://www.theguardian.com/business/2016/oct/05/talktalk-hit-with-record-400k-fine-over-cyber-attack*.

especially when connected to the Internet, and mandated that the database be ported to a more recent or alternative version.

If that proved impossible, it would have at least ensured that the security patch made available by the vendor three years before was installed. Instead, the site went live and TalkTalk's customers lost out.

CHAPTER 8: HUMAN THREATS

Some of the biggest threats to cyber security come not from technology, but from the people who use it. 68% of organisations have observed a rise in insider attacks and, as mentioned in chapter 6, 70% actually experienced at least one insider attack in 2019.[18]

When you think about it, this should make sense – for all the different types of malware that are out there, they still need to find a way of getting into an organisation's systems. Getting an insider to inadvertently introduce it into your network by, for example, opening a malicious attachment from an email that appears to come from the CEO (in other words, by making them fall for a phishing attack) is an effective method.

This is especially true when you think about how much information is publicly available and the numbers: an attacker can easily appear more authentic by doing a little research on the normal Internet – they do not even need the dark web for this – and can try their luck on perhaps hundreds of employees and contractors. Every one of those hundreds presents a human vulnerability, and just one careless click is all an attacker needs to get in.

Furthermore, once the attacker can get in, a different type of internal threat could come into play: either the attacker steals and misuses an authorised user's credentials, or they might create a tunnel going outside your perimeter, thus bypassing your firewalls and other protective measures. In both cases,

---

[18] "2020 Insider Threat Report."

they gain access to your internal networks, which could allow them to access and exfiltrate confidential data.

8.1 Staff awareness

Protecting against human threats requires training: employees need to know how to identify phishing emails and other commonly encountered threats, and how to respond when they encounter them. Employees also need to know how to go about their daily job in a secure manner, whether that be locking filing cabinets when not in use or knowing which databases contain sensitive information and how to access them securely. Secure working does not just protect the organisation from attacks, it also helps prevent accidental damage to information and information systems by promoting a conscientious approach to daily tasks.

Training is a good defence against attacks that take advantage of human nature, but it is equally important to develop a security culture within the organisation, and an environment that supports it. Employees who are busy or stressed are less likely to remember and make use of training, and more likely to fall victim to common attacks. Training will also be of limited use if staff do not take it seriously because of a poor security culture.

The security culture you create, and the environment in which that culture operates, must be positive in order for your organisation to fully benefit. Employees who fear punishment for falling victim to an attack will be less likely to report suspected attacks, which puts your whole organisation at risk. The blame game does not help anyone.

Both staff training and building a healthy, strong security culture are discussed in more detail in 12.11.

8.2 Social engineering

Social engineering attacks have existed since the early days of human civilisation. From the ancient Greeks' use of the Trojan Horse to attack Troy, to Victor Lustig's efforts in the 1920s to sell the Eiffel Tower for scrap (twice), con artists have plied their trade and caused misery to millions throughout history.

Social engineering is a type of attack in which a person is manipulated into doing something they should not – opening an infected email attachment, or divulging sensitive information, for example. Social engineering attacks are one of the most common cyber security concerns, with 88% of respondents to Proofpoint's 2020 State of the Phish Report experiencing at least one spear phishing attack in 2019 (which is a more targeted form of phishing), and 55% falling victim to at least one successful phishing attack.[19]

Social engineering attacks come in all shapes and sizes, from the 'classic' email attachment scam to complex 'pretexting' attacks in which the attacker manufactures a convincing scenario to achieve their goal. Having said that, Proofpoint's 2019 data shows that there has been a trend for "quality over quantity" when it comes to phishing.[20]

8.2.1 Phishing

The most prevalent form of social engineering attack, phishing is the act of fraudulently obtaining information, or trying to get users to act in a certain way (such as making a

---

[19] Proofpoint, "2020 State of the Phish Report", January 2020, *https://www.proofpoint.com/uk/resources/threat-reports/state-of-phish*.

[20] Ibid.

payment or downloading malware), through electronic communications that appear to be from legitimate sources. Phishing comes in a variety of flavours depending on the target and the method of execution, but the most common vector is email.

Phishing emails have come a long way since the infamous 'Nigerian Prince' emails of the early 2000s. Although some phishing emails still employ poor spelling and grammar, and describe implausible scenarios that demand the urgent provision of your bank details, many are now far more subtle and believable.

Most phishing emails are crafted to look just like an email from a legitimate sender – using the same fonts, logos and even phrasing to convince you that the email is real, and using spoofed sender addresses to further enhance the appearance of a legitimate communication. The email will invariably ask you to open an attachment or click a link – perhaps to reset your password, or to update your payment information. Do so, and you become the victim.

Links in phishing emails will appear to be legitimate, but closer examination will often highlight discrepancies such as deliberate misspelling or use of dubious subdomains. The website you visit may steal your credentials, or the attachment you open may contain a malware payload that gives the attacker access to your network. The outcome is rarely immediately visible, as in most cases this would trigger a security response – far better, in most cases, for the attack to remain hidden. This gives the attacker time to escalate their privileges, move through your networks and do maximum damage.

Historically, phishing mostly consisted of untargeted 'bulk' attacks but, as mentioned earlier, lately there has been a shift towards better quality, more targeted methods. Phishing that targets specific organisations or persons is called 'spear phishing', and often masquerades as emails from suppliers or other trusted third parties. A further variant is 'whaling', which targets senior executives with well-crafted emails designed to appeal to them specifically – perhaps masquerading as a contract dispute or escalated customer complaint. The flipside of whaling is business email compromise (BEC), in which the phishing email appears to come from a senior executive.

Other variants of phishing include phishing by phone or Voice over Internet Protocol (VoIP) ('vishing') and by text message ('smishing'). With enough effort, a determined attacker can compromise any communication medium to deliver their phishing attacks.

8.2.2 Social media

Social media may be a great tool for communicating and sharing information, but like any online activity, it comes with its own set of risks. We happily share our photos, locations and sensitive information with little thought for our own security or privacy. We also rarely consider the risks our social media activity might pose to others – whether friends, family or the organisations we work for.

When sharing information on social media, it is important to consider how that information might be used. Password reset functions, for example, often have a security question as an additional layer of security: your mother's maiden name, your first pet or a school you attended. You may think your answer to that question is something that few people would know, but if you have posted family details or photos of pets on social media, or signed up to a school reunion page, then attackers can find that information with relatively little effort.

Information shared on social media is of immense value, but passive information collection is not the only risk. 'Catfishing' – the use of a fake profile to elicit sensitive information from a person – is common on social media platforms, including dating apps and websites. The fake profile will begin an apparently innocuous conversation to gain the recipient's trust, then over time, will manipulate the recipient into providing more information.

Catfishing is frequently used to perform reconnaissance on an organisation, eliciting information from the organisation's employees in preparation for an attack. It is also used to steal credentials or even whole identities.

Social media apps can also be a source of risk, even when developed by large organisations such as LinkedIn and Facebook. In 2017, security researchers discovered that it was possible to send malicious files as attachments to LinkedIn messages despite the platform's security restrictions.[21] Just one year later, security researchers identified a vulnerability in Facebook's Messenger app that allowed criminal hackers to expose a user's contact list and messages.[22]

---

[21] Check Point, "Is Malware Hiding in Your Resume? Vulnerability in LinkedIn Messenger Would Have Allowed Malicious File Transfer", August 2017, *https://blog.checkpoint.com/2017/08/18/malware-hiding-resume-vulnerability-linkedin-messenger-allowed-malicious-file-transfer/*.

[22] Ron Masas, "Patched Facebook Vulnerability Could Have Exposed Private Information About You and Your Friends", *Imperva*, November 2018, *https://www.imperva.com/blog/facebook-privacy-bug/*.

To defend against social media attacks, develop a policy on the use of social media on work computers. Such a policy should prohibit employees from posting sensitive information about your organisation on social media and might also ban installing social media apps on mobiles and other portable devices. Train employees to understand the risks posed by social media to help them stay safe at home as well as at work.

8.3 Remote working

The freedom to work from home, on the train or in another country entirely is a huge boon to employees and employers – and vital in 2020, when we had to maintain social distancing to minimise Covid-19 infection rates – but it brings with it a host of security risks. Controlling those risks is more challenging because remote employees operate outside your organisation's logical perimeter (the boundaries within which your networks and information reside). Extending those boundaries without effective controls makes your security more permeable than it would otherwise be – if your employees can access confidential information remotely, so can attackers.

Of all the risks associated with remote working, particularly when doing so from a public area, loss or theft is probably the most common. Mobile devices such as phones or laptops are easily lost or forgotten while travelling, and theft has long been a risk for portable equipment of any kind. Your remote working policy should contain requirements for the handling of mobile devices while off-premises: do not leave devices unattended, especially in public places; do not store devices in vehicles, especially visibly; when in a hotel, make use of the safe provided; etc. In any case, portable devices should be encrypted (see 12.7), so even if one is lost or stolen, the confidentiality of your information remains intact. Ideally, it should also be possible to remotely wipe a device.

Remote working invariably requires the worker to connect to the Internet. Free Wi-Fi is available in a wide range of places, from trains to cafés, but using it can be risky. Criminal hackers can create false wireless access points (WAPs) to harvest credentials and other sensitive network traffic, while poorly secured networks can expose you to malware and man-in-the-middle (MITM) attacks. The safest option is to prohibit such devices from connecting to public Wi-Fi at all, but this is not always possible. If the use of a public Wi-Fi network cannot be avoided, the next best option is to connect to a virtual private network (VPN). A VPN allows you to connect securely to another network via the Internet, preventing anyone monitoring Wi-Fi traffic from intercepting the data you send or receive.

USB charging is another potential source of risk. Most USB sockets allow data transfer as well as power transfer, and cyber security professionals have already demonstrated that it is possible to deliver malware and even record the screens of devices connected to chargers.[23] As such, you might want to consider using USB data blockers (a USB socket with the data transfer pins removed) and disabling USB ports on laptops and other portable devices.

One vulnerability associated with remote working is something that many of us would not give much thought to – eavesdropping. Most of us assume a certain degree of

---

[23] Catalin Cimpanu, "Officials warn about the dangers of using public USB charging stations", *ZDNet*, November 2019, *https://www.zdnet.com/article/officials-warn-about-the-dangers-of-using-public-usb-charging-stations/*.

privacy, even in public spaces, and we discuss sensitive topics openly in bars, restaurants, etc., assuming no one is really listening.

Sometimes, though, someone is listening. An executive who commutes via train and regularly takes business calls during the journey is a prime target for reconnaissance by hostile actors. An attacker could take the same train and sit close enough to be able to hear the executive's conversations. Given enough time, the attacker might glean useful information about the executive's organisation – information that can then be used to carry out a more technical attack. Although such disclosures are naturally difficult to control, you can ensure that your cyber security training includes advice not to discuss confidential matters in public places.

'Shoulder-surfing', where someone reads your screen over your shoulder, is another potential problem when working remotely in public places. Although the easiest way of mitigating this risk is simply to sit somewhere that prevents someone from viewing your screen, this is not always an option. To add another layer of protection, provide users with privacy screens for laptops and similar devices. These reduce the effective viewing angle of the screen, making it impossible for the screen to be viewed from the side.

8.4 Human threat example: WannaCry

In 2017, a major ransomware attack struck systems across the globe. The program, known as 'WannaCry', infected a huge number of systems across organisations including Nissan and FedEx. In the UK, the NHS was hit hard, with more than 70,000 computers and items of medical equipment affected in 80 NHS organisations. The attack saw more than 19,000 operations cancelled and cost the NHS an estimated

£92 million (about $118 million)[24] – all because someone clicked a malicious link or opened a malicious file.

The WannaCry ransomware spread by exploiting a vulnerability in the Windows Server Message Block (SMB) protocol that allowed code to be executed on the target system. The US National Security Agency (NSA) is believed to have identified the vulnerability as far back as 2012, but instead of notifying Microsoft, it instead developed a tool to exploit the vulnerability, code-named 'EternalBlue'.[25]

At some point – it is not clear when – NSA realised that EternalBlue may have been stolen. Believing the usefulness of the tool to be diminishing and concerned for the potential impact if the exploit were to be used at scale, NSA informed Microsoft of the vulnerability. Microsoft responded quickly, releasing a critical security patch for all supported operating systems in March 2017.

In April 2017, the criminal hacker group known as the 'Shadow Brokers' released the code for EternalBlue. In May 2017, WannaCry hit the headlines.

WannaCry spread as far and as fast as it did because of a combination of unclear incident response procedures and the

---

[24] UK Department of Health & Social Care, "Securing cyber resilience in health and care: October 2018 update", October 2018, *https://www.gov.uk/government/publications/securing-cyber-resilience-in-health-and-care-october-2018-update*.

[25] Ellen Nakashima and Craig Timberg, "NSA officials worried about the day its potent hacking tool would get loose. Then it did.", *The Washington Post*, May 2017, *https://www.washingtonpost.com/business/technology/nsa-officials-worried-about-the-day-its-potent-hacking-tool-would-get-loose-then-it-did/2017/05/16/50670b16-3978-11e7-a058-ddbb23c75d82_story.html*.

failure to apply security patches promptly. Although individual NHS organisations began informing NHS Digital, the police and others that something was wrong on the morning of the first attacks, there was no coordinated response until that evening.[26]

Microsoft's March 2017 security patch applied to all supported OS including Windows 7 – yet Windows 7 accounted for around 98% of WannaCry infections worldwide.[27] None of the 80 affected NHS organisations had installed the patch, despite advice to do so issued by NHS Digital in April 2017.[28]

The WannaCry attack illustrates both the importance of effective patch management (see 12.6.2), and how quickly an attack can spread without a tested and effective incident response plan (see 14.1.2). If the patch had been applied and the response better coordinated, the attack might have been prevented entirely. At the very least, it would have had much less of an impact.

---

[26] National Audit Office, "Investigation: WannaCry cyber attack and the NHS", April 2018, *https://www.nao.org.uk/wp-content/uploads/2017/10/Investigation-WannaCry-cyber-attack-and-the-NHS.pdf*.

[27] Russell Brandom, "Almost all WannaCry victims were running Windows 7 – Windows XP was 'insignificant,' researchers say", *The Verge*, May 2017, *https://www.theverge.com/2017/5/19/15665488/wannacry-windows-7-version-xp-patched-victim-statistics*.

[28] William Smart, "Lessons learned review of the WannaCry Ransomware Cyber Attack", Department of Health & Social Care, February 2018, *https://www.england.nhs.uk/wp-content/uploads/2018/02/lessons-learned-review-wannacry-ransomware-cyber-attack-cio-review.pdf*.

CHAPTER 9: PHYSICAL THREATS

Physical threats are an often-neglected aspect of cyber security, yet they can affect organisations every bit as much as technological threats. Cyber and information security must incorporate physical security to be truly effective – it is no good protecting sensitive data with an array of technological controls if someone can simply walk in the building and take it. An attacker might also want to gain physical access to your offices to, for example, install a keylogger or another type of hardware.

9.1 Physical entry threats

A common way for attackers to gain entry is tailgating. Tailgating is a social engineering technique used to gain access to secure buildings and areas by playing off people's innate need to be helpful and liked. All you need to successfully tailgate is a little preparation to ensure you do not look out of place, and the ability to think on your feet.

One tailgating tactic is for an attacker to join employees on their cigarette break pretending to be someone who recently joined the company (which conveniently explains why they do not have ID or key cards), then follow them inside when they finish. Advance reconnaissance improves the success rate of such attacks – dropping a name or two during the conversation, or mentioning a project or some other 'inside' information helps reinforce the illusion that the attacker is a real employee.

To avoid talking to legitimate staff altogether, another tactic is to pretend to be on a phone call – while a trained security guard should still stop them to ask who they are and why they are there, people otherwise tend to be too polite to interrupt an apparent conversation, and instead simply silently hold open the door. All the attacker needs to do is nod or mouth their thanks.[29]

Some physical entry threats are more overt. Attackers can pretend to be visiting a member of staff, or pose as a maintenance worker, and gain entry that way. Such attackers will likely refuse escorts, perhaps claiming they are running late, or that they already know the way. As soon as they are left alone, they can begin their attack. These attacks are often used to install physical hardware such as USB keyloggers or keyboard, video, mouse (KVM) switches that are designed to allow a user to operate multiple computers from a single workstation. Alternatively, they may try to gain access to your information, either in hard copy or by exfiltrating it from a computer.

There are steps you can take to protect against tailgating and other physical entry threats, which are discussed in more detail in 12.3.

9.2 Physical security and mobile devices

Tailgating is not the only area in which human and physical threats overlap. When using mobile devices, particularly when working remotely, the risk of loss or theft discussed earlier clearly is a physical as well as a human security concern. How to mitigate this type of risk is discussed in more detail in 12.3.5.

---

[29] IT Governance consultants, when on site with a client, have genuinely used this and similar tactics to test the client's physical security, with a worrying amount of success.

There are, however, more novel ways in which physical threats can be combined with social engineering techniques. For example, an attacker might leave an unmarked USB device lying around where your employees are likely to encounter it – perhaps in the car park, or near an entryway – in the hope that an employee sees it, picks it up and plugs it into their computer to find out what is on it.

This attack type is surprisingly successful. A 2016 study found that at least 45% of USB drives left lying around a university campus had one or more files opened, and 98% were removed from the drop locations.[30] It is an attack type that plays on our curiosity and natural tendency to be altruistic (most users picked up the devices intending to return them to the owner), and can be very difficult to defend against.

Any unidentified mobile device found on or near the premises can be a threat. Train employees to hand in found mobile devices and to understand the risks that malicious devices can pose (staff training is discussed in more detail in 12.11). Train your IT department to test any found devices on an air-gapped, bare-bones test system so that any malware on the device cannot spread across networks, and to minimise hardware damage if the device turns out to be a USB killer (when connected, this small device sends high-voltage power surges that can damage hardware components).

---

[30] Matthew Tischer et al., "Users really do plug in USB drives they find", *2016 IEEE Symposium on Security and Privacy (SP)*, May 2016, *https://elie.net/publication/users-really-do-plug-in-usb-drives-they-find/*.

9.3 Environmental threats

In Chapter 6, we discussed the example of an environmental threat – a rainstorm. Even though this type of threat is often not malicious, it can be just as catastrophic as a technical or human threat. However, like any other threat, it only presents a risk if there is a vulnerability it can exploit – a leaky roof, for example.

Extreme weather is not the only environmental threat to consider. Floods, earthquakes and fire can all do significant damage, as could neighbouring businesses in sectors such as oil or chemicals. The important thing is that you do not overlook this threat type – in 12.3.7 we discuss some of the ways in which you can address it.

9.4 Physical threat example: KVM attacks

KVM switches are devices that allow a user to switch the computer they are operating without changing keyboard, screen or mouse. KVM switches are often found in data centres, allowing operators to connect to different servers from the same workstation. KVMs from reputable manufacturers come with built-in security functions to prevent external attackers connecting to them and accessing the connected computers, which is a comfort – but what if the KVM used to attack you belongs to someone else?

KVM attacks hit the news in 2013 with a spate of attacks targeting London banks. Beginning in April 2013, an attacker entered a Barclays branch claiming to be IT support staff and attached a 3G-enabled KVM switch to bank computers. The 3G connection allowed the attacker to connect to the KVM through the Internet, giving them full control over the connected computer from a remote location. Once they had control, all they had to do was transfer money from one account to another in amounts that were sufficiently small to avoid additional scrutiny.

The attacker stole £1.25 million (about $1.6 million), £600,000 (about $770,000) of which was recovered by Barclays. In July of that year, the attacker struck another Barclays branch, resulting in the theft of £90,000 (about $115,000). This time, the KVM switch was recovered by police, but the attacker remains at large.

In September 2013, the attacker switched targets to a Santander branch. Just as before, the attacker entered the premises under the guise of IT support staff and attached another 3G-enabled KVM device to bank computers, while accomplices were waiting to transfer funds to holding accounts as they had in previous attacks. This time, however, the police were ready.

A raid carried out on an accomplice's property revealed computers in the middle of carrying out the Santander attack, along with a treasure trove of stolen credit cards, letters, usernames and passwords, and other material used to commit fraud. Police arrested the 'IT support engineer' shortly after he left the bank.[31]

The 2013 KVM attackers exploited social engineering vulnerabilities (by pretending to be IT support) to install a hardware-based threat (the 3G-enabled KVM switch). They knew enough about banking systems to ensure that the international transfers made were just below the limit that

---

[31] Kate Ferguson, "Cyber gang who stole £1.25m from banks guilty of fraud", *Evening Standard*, March 2014, *https://www.standard.co.uk/news/crime/cyber-gang-who-stole-125m-from-banks-guilty-of-fraud-9190978.html.*

would trigger additional checks, suggesting that research and reconnaissance were performed to identify the safest way of extracting the money without drawing attention (and likely to identify target branches, too).

Such 'combined' attacks are effective because they bypass many of the controls put in place to defend against them. The 3G router allowed the KVM switch to be operated over a mobile Internet connection, bypassing the bank's network security controls, while the social engineering techniques allowed the attackers to bypass physical entry controls. Protecting against combined attacks requires combined defences, or 'defence in depth', which is discussed in more detail in 12.12.8.

CHAPTER 10: THIRD-PARTY THREATS

An increasingly interconnected world requires increasingly interconnected organisations. No matter the field your organisation operates in, there is a good chance you rely on components or even whole products produced by third parties. No doubt you also share data – via email perhaps, or through a dedicated vendor portal. This connectivity brings great business benefits, but it also exposes you to new risks. The risks that directly relate to your organisation are completely within your control, but your suppliers' measures are a different matter.

10.1 Supply chain threats

The modern supply chain stretches across the globe and encompasses thousands of organisations. More data is shared across the supply chain than ever before, and although this brings increased efficiency and productivity, it also introduces risk.

Once a relatively rare occurrence, attacks carried out via the supply chain have been rising steadily, with a 2019 report by Symantec noting an increase of 78% on the previous year.[32] This increase in activity is reflected in the number of organisations suffering data breaches caused by third parties

[32] "Internet Security Threat Report (ISTR) Volume 24."

– a whopping 59% of respondents to a 2018 Ponemon Institute survey.[33]

Even if you impose extensive controls on your suppliers, attacks conducted against your organisation through your supply chain are not the only thing you need to consider. Although many supply chain attacks are explicitly designed to exploit weaknesses in a supplier's security to attack one or more of their clients, an attack intended to disrupt the supplier itself can deny you access to key systems and/or services.

10.1.1 Scale and authority problems

Defending against supply chain attacks is a major cyber security challenge. The first problem is one of scale. It is not uncommon for small- to medium-sized organisations to have more than a hundred suppliers, and for larger organisations the numbers tend to increase commensurately. 60% of respondents to the Ponemon Institute survey say they do not monitor third-party security or privacy practices because of a lack of resources, and this is likely just the tip of the iceberg.[34]

Another problem is authority. Large organisations with significant buying power find it easier to impose cyber security requirements on their suppliers, but smaller organisations often struggle. 60% of respondents to the Ponemon Institute survey said that suppliers refuse to allow independent monitoring or verification of their security and

---

[33] Ponemon Institute, "Data Risk in the Third-Party Ecosystem – Third Annual Report", November 2018, *https://promotions.opus.com/l/12092/2018-11-14/6bj4g6*.

[34] Ibid.

privacy activities, and only 23% conduct independent audits or third-party verification.[35] Furthermore, many organisations (47%) only conduct a legal or procurement review when considering a new supplier, yet these generally focus on the supplier's ability to meet production or service requirements and place little emphasis on cyber security matters.[36]

Enforcing cyber security requirements on suppliers is a thorny problem. Even in scenarios where the supplier is amenable to your requirements, they may not have the resources or expertise to achieve them. A pragmatic approach is essential – it is neither necessary nor practical for every supplier to employ extensive cyber security measures. Instead, tailor requirements to the supplier – consider the quantity and sensitivity of the information they have access to and how they access it and set requirements accordingly. Also bear in mind that a supplier does not need access to your information to create a security vulnerability – if your Internet (or power in general) goes down, for instance, you lose access to information saved in the Cloud.

At the end of the day, you have more control over your own mitigation measures than those of a supplier, so take action to reduce reliance on supplier controls by applying your own instead, where possible.

---

[35] Ponemon Institute, "Data Risk in the Third-Party Ecosystem – Third Annual Report", November 2018, *https://promotions.opus.com/l/12092/2018-11-14/6bj4g6*.

[36] Ibid.

10.1.2 Understanding data flow

Perhaps the biggest problem is understanding how much data you share with your suppliers, and what they do with it after it leaves your control. Under data protection laws such as the EU GDPR, as the data controller, you are still responsible for the data you share with data processors such as suppliers. As such, should the supplier suffer a breach, your organisation is at risk of receiving a fine (unless exceptional circumstances apply, such as the supplier not following your contractual agreement, and that non-compliance led to the breach).

To avoid such situations, performing a certain amount of due diligence is essential. 12.13.1 covers such checks in more detail.

10.1.3 Cloud services

Cloud services are increasingly prevalent in modern IT operations. They offer scalable processing and storage and can be a massive boon to organisations, yet their opacity and distance make them among the hardest systems over which to exercise effective control.

Given how difficult it can be to audit or otherwise verify the IT security of even immediate suppliers, the chances of visiting, say, Amazon's server farms to conduct a security audit are essentially zero. In many cases, you have little choice but to trust the information the Cloud provider makes available (which will be limited anyway for, ironically, security purposes). As a result, ensuring cyber security in respect of Cloud services requires research and no small amount of trust.

Having said that, you can achieve a lot by carefully reviewing your contracts/service level agreements (SLAs) – you may not be able to negotiate the terms and conditions, but you can at least make sure that you are happy with the ones offered. This is discussed in more detail in 12.13.2.

10.2 Third-party threat example: Target data breach

In 2013, US retailer Target suffered a data breach that resulted in the loss of 70 million personally identifiable information (PII) records and up to 40 million payment card credentials. A successful phishing attack on one of Target's third-party heating, ventilation and air-conditioning suppliers installed a Trojan that the supplier's limited cyber security measures failed to detect. The Trojan went undetected for long enough to capture the login credentials used to access Target's internal vendor portal.[37]

With those credentials, the attackers infiltrated Target's internal network and uploaded malware to several cash registers in Target stores, apparently to test the malware's effectiveness. Once satisfied, the attackers proceeded to upload the malware to point-of-sale (POS) devices in the majority of Target stores across the US.[38] Every time a customer used a card in an infected device, the malware accessed the device's memory, intercepting names, card numbers and other sensitive information. Once captured, the malware encrypted the information and stored it on

---

[37] Brian Krebs, "Target Hackers Broke in Via HVAC Company", *Krebs on Security*, February 2014, https://krebsonsecurity.com/2014/02/target-hackers-broke-in-via-hvac-company/.

[38] Ibid.

compromised systems within Target's internal network before sending it to the attackers.

A leaked report from a penetration test carried out after the attack laid bare a number of security issues at Target, but critically, the report found "no controls limiting [the tester's] access to any system, including devices within stores such as point of sale (POS) registers and servers".[39] Essentially, once the attackers had access to Target's network via the supplier's login, they had free rein to do as they pleased.

A few months later, Home Depot fell victim to a variant of the same malware.[40] 56 million payment cards and 53 million email addresses were disclosed in the attack, which – you guessed it – was traced back to a compromised supplier.[41]

The Target and Home Depot attacks shook US consumer confidence in large retailers, making clear that even large, trusted organisations might be putting their personal information at risk. They also marked a watershed moment in the cyber security field, as organisations began to face up

---

[39] Brian Krebs, "Inside Target Corp., Days After 2013 Breach", *Krebs on Security*, September 2015, *https://krebsonsecurity.com/2015/09/inside-target-corp-days-after-2013-breach/*.

[40] Brian Krebs, "Home Depot Hit By Same Malware as Target", *Krebs on Security*, September 2014, *https://krebsonsecurity.com/2014/09/home-depot-hit-by-same-malware-as-target/*.

[41] Tara Seals, "Home Depot: Massive Breach Happened Via Third-Party Vendor Credentials", *Infosecurity Magazine*, November 2014, *https://www.infosecurity-magazine.com/news/home-depot-breach-third-party/*.

to the risks concealed in their supply chains. Incidents such as the Ticketmaster data breach in 2018, however, suggest that there is still some way to go.[42]

---

[42] Amelia Wade, "Ticketmaster data breach: Thousands of customers may be affected", *Which?*, June 2018, *https://www.which.co.uk/news/2018/06/ticketmaster-data-breach-thousands-of-customers-may-be-affected/*.

Part 3: The CRF processes

CHAPTER 11: AN OVERVIEW OF THE CRF PROCESSES

Part 3 – by far the longest part of this book – goes into a wide range of security processes (all taken from the CRF) you might need to implement. For ease of reference, this chapter offers a short description for each of the 24 processes within our CRF, giving you a better idea of which ones you should look at further.

To break the Framework down, there are four process categories, with each process falling within one of them. Each category describes how its processes fit within the overall Framework. The four categories are:

1. **Manage and protect:**
   Deploy risk-appropriate information security measures – relying on people, processes and technology – to protect the confidentiality, integrity and availability (CIA) of your information assets, business processes and infrastructure.
2. **Identify and detect:**
   Develop a system to identify anomalies that may signify an incident through automated, continual security monitoring, with manual follow-ups.
3. **Respond and recover:**
   To be truly resilient, you need to put responsive measures in place to complete the three-pronged prevention–detection–response system. That way, if an attack succeeds despite your best efforts, you can

respond to and recover from it efficiently, prioritising your most critical functions and assets.

4. **Govern and assure:**
   Validate your security efforts, make corrections and improvements where possible, and ensure ongoing board-level oversight of and commitment to cyber security.

The processes themselves describe a set of activities at a high level. In the following four chapters, each process will be explained in more detail. To guide you, Table 2 provides a brief description and the key output of each.

Table 2: High-level Overview of all CRF Processes

Category	Process name	Process description	Key output
Chapter 12: Manage and protect	12.1 Asset management	Both IT and information assets are logged, tracked and managed throughout their lifecycle. Each asset has a defined 'owner' who is responsible for it.	A well-managed system for tracking (classes of) IT and information assets, along with useful information for each entry.
	12.2 Information security policies	Documents that state how your organisation plans to protect its physical and information assets. This should include activities to make	A set of documents, issued and approved by top management, that establish your position on information

Category	Process name	Process description	Key output
		sure policies are communicated to and understood by all staff and contractors.	security and instruct staff how to act securely.
	12.3 Physical and environmental security	The physical environment where information and information assets are kept is protected from physical intrusion by unauthorised individuals, natural or man-made disasters, and locally relevant threats.	A clearly defined physical perimeter that is protected by appropriate physical and environmental security controls to reduce the risk posed by physical and environmental threats.
	12.4 Identity and access control	Measures to ensure that the person attempting to access information and information systems (physically or logically) is who they say they are and that they are authorised to access that information.	Effective controls and policies that help verify the identity of users, prevent the misuse of privileged access rights and stop unauthorised individuals from entering the premises.
	12.5 Malware protection	Measures that protect your computer systems and information	Technical and organisational measures, including anti-

Category	Process name	Process description	Key output
		from a broad range of malware.	malware software and an anti-malware policy, that protect your organisation from malware.
	12.6 Configuration and patch management	Software and IT equipment are securely configured and kept up to date, and retired where they are no longer supported.	A systematic process for minimising vulnerabilities affecting hardware and software through secure configurations and patching.
	12.7 Encryption	Cryptographic solutions, including encryption, pseudonymisation and anonymisation, are deployed where necessary to reduce the risk to information at rest and in transit. Encryption and decryption keys are kept secure.	An encryption policy that makes clear when to use encryption and how keys are protected, and appropriate technical measures to enforce the policy.
	12.8 System security	Systems should be designed with security in mind from the earliest stages. Deploying	Security by design processes, including regular reviews.

Category	Process name	Process description	Key output
		third-party systems should also take security by design into account.	
	12.9 Network and communications security	The corporate network should be designed with security in mind, using appropriate technologies and processes such as segmentation and segregation.	Defined security zones that meet the organisation's security requirements, with appropriate technical measures (such as firewalls and demilitarised zones (DMZs)) in place to form internal perimeters, as well as the external perimeter, covering the entire corporate network.
	12.10 Security competence and training	Staff with a security role or security responsibilities have the right competences and qualifications to carry out their duties. These security activities can also be outsourced.	Processes for identifying, developing and maintaining necessary competence.

Category	Process name	Process description	Key output
	12.11 Staff awareness training	Employees receive regular cyber security awareness training, and know how to recognise and respond to security threats. Security should also be embedded in the organisation's culture.	Established staff awareness training programme with clearly defined and measurable learning objectives.
	12.12 Compreh-ensive risk management programme	Identifying, assessing and responding to cyber and information security risks in a structured and methodical manner, as part of a wider risk management programme.	Comprehensive and structured risk assessments conducted on a regular basis.
	12.13 Supply chain risk management	Steps are taken, including due diligence checks and appropriate contracts, to ensure the entire supply chain, including physical suppliers, software vendors and Cloud service providers, is secure.	Processes and checklists for checking information-sharing rules and security responsibilities are adequate and clear, and legally enforceable.

Category	Process name	Process description	Key output
Chapter 13: Identify and detect	13.1 Threat and vulnerability intelligence	Receiving intelligence on threats, vulnerabilities and security measures from feeds likely to be relevant to the organisation to keep up with the ever-changing cyber landscape and help inform, in particular, advance and post-incident detection activities.	Following relevant threat bulletins and using them as inputs for your detection activities, as well as a programme of regular vulnerability scanning and penetration testing.
	13.2 Security monitoring	The organisation's systems and networks are continually monitored for anomalies, through a combination of automated tools and human input to try to detect incidents as quickly as possible, and continually logged so incidents can be identified and investigated.	Strategically placed sensors that collect data, which is analysed by automated tools in real time, followed up by human input. Collected data is stored so it can serve as evidence in a later investigation if needed.
Chapter 14: Respond and recover	14.1 Incident response management	In recognition of the risk that your preventive measures can fail no matter how strong, you	An incident response team, and clear and tested incident

Category	Process name	Process description	Key output
		need to be able to react to and mitigate incidents effectively. To do so, you need to take preparatory steps to have the best chance of making the right decisions when speed is of the essence.	response plans and procedures.
	14.2 ICT continuity management	Business-critical ICT functions should be treated like any other primary business asset, and be resilient in the event of disruption, with risk-appropriate measures put in place to ensure continuity.	Agreed thresholds and timescales for recovering ICT functions following an incident, along with appropriate fallback measures.
	14.3 Business continuity management	Disruptions of varying nature and scale, both foreseeable and unexpected, inevitably occur in business. Business continuity management (BCM) helps you to prepare for them, ensuring that you can continue to operate – even if at a lower	Business continuity plans, covering multiple broad scenarios that are based on objective business impact analysis (BIA) and risk assessment, and have been tested to ensure they work as intended and staff know

Category	Process name	Process description	Key output
		level than normal – no matter what you are faced with.	what is expected of them.
Chapter 15: Govern and assure	15.1 Formal information security management programme	This metaprocess, binding together and unifying the other CRF processes, entails a structured approach to securing information assets across the organisation, taking people, processes and technologies into account. As you establish the processes and implement controls, you should also decide how you will measure and monitor their performance to validate their effectiveness.	A clear management structure; defined scope; roles and responsibilities; documented policies and procedures; and a strategy for measurement.
	15.2 Continual improvement process	Security measures should be regularly reviewed, and improved or adapted where necessary, in a continual, cyclical improvement process.	Formal review and planning stages for existing processes, preferably in addition to a formal 'lessons learned' process. Some organisations

Category	Process name	Process description	Key output
			may also want to adopt a more widespread improvement model, or extend one already used to include cyber security.
	15.3 Board-level commitment and involvement	Considering that cyber security is an increasingly important prerequisite for doing business, the potential impact of breaches and the need for a top-down approach to make the cyber security implementation project successful, the board and/or top management should take an active – and visible – interest in cyber security.	The board and/or top management visibly takes cyber security seriously by allocating sufficient resources and, where necessary, offering direction and support to cyber security efforts.
	15.4 Governance structure and processes	As the effectiveness and reliability of an organisation's IT products and services is usually of clear strategic importance to an organisation's ability to do business, intellectual capital	Identified directors are accountable for the delivery of the organisation's IT products and services, and regularly evaluate, direct

Category	Process name	Process description	Key output
		and ICT should be overseen by its governing body.	and monitor IT-related activities.
	15.5 Internal audit	The organisation's information security measures are independently reviewed for their effectiveness on a regular basis, providing the assurance that they are fit for purpose and working correctly. The audit results are reviewed and assessed by senior management.	A programme of regular internal audits, conducted objectively by an impartial auditor, with results reported to management.
	15.6 External certification/ validation	If there is a business need to provide evidence of the strength of your security, such as meeting contractual requirements or providing assurances to stakeholders, you should consider the value of seeking external certification.	Decide on whether to pursue external certification based on your security needs and objectives.

The final chapter of this part of the book talks about the CRF's four maturity levels – as mentioned in the introduction, we recommend only implementing the processes you need, and only to the lowest level of maturity that meets your needs. This approach will help keep your cyber security activities manageable as well as give you the best return on investment.

CHAPTER 12: MANAGE AND PROTECT

> Deploy risk-appropriate information security measures – relying on people, processes and technology – to protect the CIA of your information assets, business processes and infrastructure.

'Manage and protect', the first and largest process category of the CRF, consists of activities that are central to managing cyber security and protecting the organisation from threats. Of course, in order for your defensive measures to be effective, you need to know what those threats are. By this we do not mean in a generic way, as discussed in part 2 of this book, but specifically those that apply to you. You need to understand who might attack you and how, and what their motivations are.

What line of business are you in? Is it likely, for instance, that politically or socially motivated individuals or groups (hacktivists) would target you? What data do you hold? Who might want that data (and is prepared to commit a crime in order to obtain it)? What methods are they likely to use? For each attack type, where are your weak points?

It also helps to have a clear idea of exactly what incidents you are trying to prevent. Everyone wants to avoid adverse consequences, but the incidents that can specifically damage *your* organisation operationally, financially and/or reputationally are unique. The information you hold is not the only asset you need to protect – there are also, for example, critical business processes that you must seek to preserve, and websites that need to stay live. Furthermore, not all information is equal in value and, to make matters more complicated, the same information may have a value that changes over time – information about new products and services, for instance, is far more valuable when not yet available in the public domain. Your regulatory or contractual requirements may also inform your priorities.[43]

Understanding what assets you must protect will help you determine the likely attacks or threats you may face, as well as how your assets might be compromised (in effect, this is risk management, which is discussed in more detail in 12.12). From there, you can make far more informed decisions about the necessary security processes and controls to implement.

As discussed in 5.1, bear in mind that each solution requires some sort of trade-off, with some bigger or more intrusive than others. Some solutions are more expensive than others, but might be easier to implement. Others might be cheaper, but require a bigger sacrifice in convenience or privacy. There are solutions that only reduce the impact of an incident or only the likelihood of one, and others that achieve both. Ultimately, security is all about considering the trade-offs, and deciding which are worth making. It is about determining your needs and making sensible decisions about how to meet them without making unpalatable sacrifices. Clearly, budget is a factor, but so is time, resources, convenience, flexibility and privacy. At the end of the day, no security solution is perfect or foolproof, but making

[43] Table 1 (see 5.3) provides an overview of which CRF processes can help you meet a number of common requirements.

strategic decisions can make the trade-offs worth the cost, financially or otherwise.

Whatever decisions you make, remember that security needs to be considered from three aspects: people, processes and technology (also see 5.2). Installing better locks on doors has little use when people do not use them, and updating your password policy to force stronger passwords is not an effective solution if people write them down on a notepad or sticky note next to their computer. Whatever solutions you choose must also be maintained: installing a sophisticated anti-malware solution only remains effective if someone keeps it up to date, for instance.

Finally, keep in mind that in order to secure information, you need to protect its CIA (also see chapter 2). In other words, the information must only be accessible to those who need access to it; protected from unauthorised modification, destruction and loss; and accessible to authorised persons as and when necessary. It is a common mistake to only consider the confidentiality of information, forgetting that if the information has been wrongly altered (breach of integrity) or is not accessible when you need it (breach of availability), that information has lost its value, and the matter needs to be deemed a security incident, even if the information has not actually fallen into the wrong hands (breach of confidentiality).

12.1 Asset management

Both IT and information assets are logged, tracked and managed throughout their lifecycle. Each asset has a defined 'owner' who is responsible for it.

Key output: A well-managed system for tracking (classes of) IT and information assets, along with useful information for each entry.

Effective cyber security starts with protecting your IT and information assets. After all, in today's information economy, your organisation's intellectual capital (often stored digitally) is probably your most critical asset, and determines how you set yourself apart from your competitors. Any information valuable to your business is, by definition, an information asset.

However, before you can protect either, you need to determine exactly what assets you have – both physical and intangible – and who is responsible for them. Compiling and maintaining a detailed asset inventory is a good way of achieving that.

12.1.1 Benefits of an asset inventory

Putting together an asset inventory as part of determining the scope of your implementation project (our eight-step approach suggests doing this in step 3; see chapter 20) will prove a worthwhile investment, as it will save considerable time, effort and money further down the line – for instance, a risk assessment will be easier and quicker to conduct when you know what assets you have and where they are. It will also produce more accurate results, which will enable you to protect your assets and organisation more effectively.

Additionally, by talking to people across the organisation to identify assets, you encourage cultural change and improve staff awareness of both cyber security and asset management. This can improve staff vigilance, which will ultimately strengthen your cyber defences.

Finally, having a comprehensive and suitably detailed asset register can help your organisation with a whole host of other activities. For instance, if you have some idea how often assets such as computers need to be replaced, or can estimate the attrition rate on losing portable devices or removable media, you can better plan your finances and identify areas where costs can be saved. Equally, if you already have an asset inventory for other purposes, it can provide a strong basis for an information asset inventory.

12.1.2 The asset inventory

Although the core output of asset management is likely the same for most organisations – an asset inventory or asset register – the way that inventory is presented and stored can significantly vary according to the organisation's size and complexity, as well as how many and what activities it intends to use the inventory for. You could use a spreadsheet, a database or software that tracks assets and/or classes of asset. Each entry should also specify certain characteristics, such as classification and location, and needs to identify an owner – the person responsible for managing the asset. 12.1.4 discusses these characteristics in more depth.

Note that you are not necessarily tracking every individual item – particularly for large or complex organisations, that would quickly become untenable. Even entries such as in the list below can be sufficient, as long as you also provide the characteristics for each:

- Desktop computer – Windows
- Desktop computer – Mac
- Mobile phone – Android
- Mobile phone – iOS
- Etc.

Alternatively, depending on your needs and budget, you might want to take a broader approach, for example:

- Desktop computer
- Mobile devices (laptop, phone and tablet)
- Etc.

There is no 'right' approach, as long as you choose one suitable for your needs and apply it consistently. The method you choose is also likely to evolve as you gain a better understanding of your information assets, environment and cyber security needs (or if any of them change).

12.1.3 Identifying assets

Although computers, mobile devices and other hardware are a good starting point, your IT assets extend far beyond these. However, remember that your focus is information and cyber security – keyboards and mice are not particularly interesting, and even the computer itself is usually of limited value, but the data held on it and its access to your internal networks are often critical to your company's survival.

Identifying information assets may prove challenging despite their fairly straightforward definition (any information valuable to your business), as you may have to track down forgotten servers or databases, check physical as well as digital locations and establish undocumented employee knowledge.

Besides hardware, software, networks, information and information systems, etc., you may also want to record assets such as organisational sites or structure, important processes and personnel. Even though these are less obviously labelled as 'IT' or 'information' assets, they clearly impact the security of those assets, so it is worth treating processes, personnel, etc. in a similar way to your 'proper' IT and information assets.

Additionally, identifying assets such as processes and personnel will help your cyber security project in later stages. For instance:

- In a risk assessment, processes and staff may introduce or mitigate risks.
- In a BIA, the impact on processes may be a key factor in measuring business disruption (also see 14.3.1).
- From a data protection perspective, recording your data processing activities as processes in your inventory will be of considerable benefit when conducting a data protection or privacy impact assessment. Keeping such records of your processing activities may also be a regulatory requirement in itself,[44] as well as help you meet further requirements (for risk or impact assessments, for example).

Depending on your needs, you may also find it valuable to classify assets as 'primary' or 'supporting'. This involves

---

[44] As an example, the EU GDPR mandates 'records of processing activities' for organisations meeting specific criteria as documented in Article 30.

distinguishing the core processes and information of a given activity (primary assets) from the assets that support those core processes and/or information (supporting assets). Such supporting assets could include hardware, software and personnel, and may have vulnerabilities that, if exploited, could impair the primary assets your business activities depend on.

All these considerations will help you establish the boundaries of what you consider an asset.

To actually identify tangible assets, procurement information can help you get a head start, but it is important to be aware that you cannot rely on those records alone to complete your inventory, as they may not go far enough back. After all, it is not uncommon for organisations to rely on technology well over five years old and there may be a limit to how far back detailed procurement records go. Furthermore, procurement information will not cover all intangible assets, nor provide full details of external information systems. It may also be spread across business areas and not held in one central unit.

External assets are easy to overlook, but are a key asset to include in your inventory. For example, if you use a Cloud service, you may well store personal data or important information on there that requires protection. Given that the Cloud servers may well be located abroad, this could also present other territorial or cross-border issues. Remote working and bring your own device (BYOD) policies may also present additional security challenges, and may make just identifying all portable hardware a much harder task. However, in the right organisational culture and with management support, sending out an all-employee email that asks employees what company equipment they believe they are responsible for can go a long way.

Appendix 1 of this book contains an asset checklist to help you get started.

12.1.4 Completing the inventory

Besides identifying the actual asset and logging it in your inventory, you will also need to record some additional details, such as:

- Asset owner;
- Classification (reflecting the sensitivity/importance of the information);
- Asset identifier;
- Asset category (e.g. 'hardware', 'portable device', 'software'); and
- Valuation.

You may also want to add further details, such as type, version number (particularly for software), operator, location (physical or digital), expiry or replacement dates, links to operating instructions, etc. Exactly what information you should record will depend on your needs and what else you use your inventory for, but asset owner is an absolute minimum. In many cases, classification will also be extremely valuable to record. For data protection purposes, you may also want to record the type of PII you hold, for instance, sensitive data, children's data, criminal data, etc.

Asset owner

As soon as an asset is created or obtained, management should appoint someone to be responsible for managing it across its lifecycle, including ensuring that it is properly inventoried, appropriately classified and protected, and deleted or destroyed in line with procedure. That owner can delegate tasks as appropriate, but will still be responsible for that asset.

Classification

To distinguish between different levels of sensitivity and/or importance of the information at hand, you need to use a classification system such as 'confidential', 'restricted', 'private' and 'public'. The names and number of levels are not particularly important, as long as you use your classification system consistently, with clearly defined levels that take into account legal requirements, sensitivity and value. Each level must also stipulate security requirements for accessing and handling the asset. Remember that your classification system can only work effectively if all employees are aware of the different classifications and what they mean.

Asset identifier

To make sure you identify each asset – especially devices – individually, as well as to avoid duplication, you could introduce some sort of unique identifier. This could be as simple as the manufacturer's serial number, but you could also introduce asset numbers through physical labels (although that may present issues if the label is removed).

Asset category

The way assets are categorised will vary per organisation. Whether those categories are very broad (e.g. 'hardware') or narrow ('mobile phone'), the key thing is to apply them consistently within your inventory.

Valuation

It may be useful to include valuation estimates in your inventory, particularly to support impact and risk assessments. A straightforward approach is to use clearly defined scales, which could be based on monetary values such as >£1,000, £1,000–£10,000, etc., while abstract bands such as 'low', 'medium', 'high', etc. can be useful where assets have a non-monetary value.

In any case, terms should be unambiguously defined and consistently used, particularly as each asset owner may have different ideas about valuation.

12.2 Information security policies

> Documents that state how your organisation plans to protect its physical and information assets. This should include activities to make sure policies are communicated to and understood by all staff and contractors.
>
> **Key output:** A set of documents, issued and approved by top management, that establish your position on information security and instruct staff how to act securely.

In essence, policies are company-wide directions to do – or prohibit – certain things. They are a statement of intent and, coupled with documented procedures, which set out in more practical terms how the policies are applied, are invaluable to your cyber security project. Policies set out the rules and boundaries your organisation operates within (based on various influences, such as legal requirements) that can influence and even direct staff behaviour, while procedures guide employees in specific situations, such as having to report a potential breach or setting up user accounts. Policies clearly demonstrate your organisation's position on and attitude towards security, which can in turn help build – and enforce – a security culture (see 12.11.5) throughout your organisation.

Another benefit of drafting and reviewing policies and, in particular, procedures is that you naturally improve your information security awareness and knowledge as you talk to individuals across the business and check how things are really done. This will also give you a better idea of how policies affect procedures. Through that process, you may also collaboratively develop more efficient procedures, and encourage staff vigilance as you talk to people around the company to gather information, and clarify responsibilities and accountability. This may lead to a naturally iterative approach where continual improvement is abundant (also see 15.2), and help you deal with the rest of your implementation project more quickly and with a greater degree of confidence.

A good and properly enforced policy can prove a more effective way of changing staff behaviour than sophisticated technological measures (although remember that you need all three – people, processes and technology – for your overall security programme to be truly effective). It is important, however, to view drafting policies and procedures as an ongoing process, not a one-off effort. Your organisation's approach to doing things will almost certainly evolve with time as you gain experience or new insights, so your documented instructions should be reviewed and updated in line with those changes.

15.1 covers effective policies and procedures in more detail, including tips on how to create them.

12.2.1 The overarching information security policy

You are likely to end up with a set of policies that form part of your information security implementation project, with one overarching information security policy and subsidiary policies that fall out of that policy, such as a password policy (see 12.4.4) and a patching policy (see 12.6.2). You will probably also have further documentation derived from those policies, such as procedures and records.

There are significant benefits to this type of hierarchical approach. Having one central policy that clearly links to your security objectives, has visible support from senior management and links to further, more specific documents will offer the best balance of coherence and usability, since your alternatives are splitting everything up into lots of separate documents without a clear hierarchy or structure, or putting everything into one enormous document that is difficult to read and likely avoided by staff as a result.

12.2.2 Policy content

Although the information security policy is necessarily a high-level and relatively abstract document, it should still be specific about some information key to your implementation project, such as:

- The scope of your project;
- Your organisation's context;
- Stakeholder needs, including relevant legal and contractual requirements; and
- The strategic aims and objectives of your information security programme.

As mentioned earlier, it is important to regularly review your policy – ideally at least annually – and when your circumstances change.

You also need to secure senior management support by getting them to approve the information security policy – in fact, the CEO or managing director should be signing it off. If senior management clearly take security seriously, staff are much more likely to follow suit, and more resources for information security will likely be made available. The policy should be published internally and communicated to all staff and contractors under management's authority. The policy should also be made available to any third parties upon request.

12.2.3 Establishing your information security objectives

Information security objectives are essentially what initiated your whole implementation project and the information security programme you later need to maintain (otherwise, the work you put in now will go to waste) – in other words, they are your goals for cyber security. As such, they are also a means of assessing your progress and checking if what you are doing is actually working, or if you need to change your approach.

An organisation's objectives heavily depend on its context (discussed in 12.2.4) – are you simply meeting regulatory or contractual requirements? Are you trying to match or stand out from your competitors? Whatever your goals, they will shape how you tackle your implementation project. We will discuss establishing information security objectives for your information security programme in more detail in step 4 of our eight-step approach to implementation.

12.2.4 Determining the scope and context

As you determine your scope, you need to make sure you at least account for business characteristics and organisational structure, location(s), assets and technology, since they may all be assets you need to protect or factors that may impair your assets if not properly secured. Your asset inventory (see 12.1) can give you a starting point.

However, there are more points to consider, including your business needs and objectives, as well as the needs or requirements of interested parties, which may include employees, contractors, customers, suppliers, partners, shareholders, regulators and auditors. You should also consider the business environment you operate in and any relevant trends – if, for example, competitors tend to have strong security in place (and advertise the fact), you probably should too. On the other hand, you may want to use your positive attitude towards strong security as a means of standing out from the competition.

We will discuss determining the context and scope for your overall implementation project – and, by extension, content for your information security policy – in more detail in steps 1–3 of our eight-step approach (see chapters 18–20).

12.2.5 Fitting the policy into the wider implementation project

Since this policy encompasses your overall information and cyber security project, and takes into account your legal, contractual and business requirements, it is important to draft your information security policy (or policies) at an early stage.

However, you should view the process as an iterative one, particularly if your organisation is large or complex – for instance, in our eight-step approach, we spread the drafting work across multiple early steps, and incorporate policy reviews and revisions in the final step.

12.3 Physical and environmental security

The physical environment where information and information assets are kept is protected from physical intrusion by unauthorised individuals, natural or man-made disasters, and locally relevant threats.

Key output: A clearly defined physical perimeter that is protected by appropriate physical and environmental security controls to reduce the risk posed by physical and environmental threats.

Information security is not just about protecting yourself from attacks conducted over the Internet, but also about not allowing unauthorised individuals onto the premises, who may compromise your information or information systems – there is little point protecting sensitive data with an array of technological controls if someone can simply walk in the building and take it (see chapter 9 for a full discussion of physical threats). Equally, you need to protect yourself from environmental threats that may impact the integrity or availability of your information, such as natural disasters and fires. There could also be a political and/or social component to physical threats, such as civil unrest or crime.

Critical or sensitive information and information systems should be housed in secure areas, such as your offices. Those areas need a defined perimeter, which should be your primary focus in terms of physical defences: protecting that perimeter with physical barriers, access controls and other measures should prevent intruders from getting in, which will in turn protect whatever information and information systems you keep within that perimeter.

However, keeping your premises secure requires some other considerations. You need to ensure that confidential information or activities are not visible or audible from the outside, whether to a passer-by (see 12.3.3), a dumpster-diver going through your bins (see 12.3.4) or in shared offices (see 12.3.2).

Where the information is particularly sensitive or critical, you may want to use more than one barrier, so the failure of one does not necessarily constitute a breach of security (see 12.12.8). To reduce the risk further and where practicable, it may be a good idea to ensure that buildings do not obviously identify their purposes so it is difficult to guess what information processing activities take place there. Where this is not possible, you should at least avoid indicating what activities take place where, including by making any internal directories not publicly accessible.

12.3.1 Defining a secure perimeter

A site or floor plan that identifies the area to be secured (i.e. where your information and information systems are located, such as your organisation's premises) is a good place to start. Such a plan may tell you what physical barriers (walls, gates, etc.) are already in place, which you can incorporate into your security perimeter. To visualise the full perimeter, draw a continuous line around the premises on the site plan such that all assets you need to protect sit within that area.

You should also pay attention to the following:

- Make sure that your exterior walls, roof and flooring are all of solid construction. False ceilings in particular may introduce a multitude of threats.
- Note all external doors and windows on your plan, including fire escapes, and secure them with appropriate access controls (see 12.4.8) and other measures (such as alarms and bars in front of windows) as necessary. Internal entry points to more sensitive areas, such as server rooms, should receive the same treatment.
- Ensure there are no unaddressed gaps in your physical perimeter – things such as skylights, air-conditioning vents and lift shafts may all be more susceptible to a break-in, so assess their risk carefully and put appropriate measures in place.

As with most security controls, it is important to balance practicalities (in this case accessibility) with security. This means, for example, not using multiple layers of controls where one would suffice, and making sensible choices for your access controls. Using traditional lock and key for an area shared with many people, for instance, is not very convenient, since it requires many keys to be issued or some employees to regularly interrupt their work to answer the door. It also risks doors being left unlocked or wedged open, defeating the purpose of the access control.

Also remember that an unauthorised individual does not have to be an intruder: even where a visitor or staff have been authorised to enter the premises, that authorisation is probably limited to certain areas. Those areas have likely been determined by the information stored within them. This too has design considerations: semi-public areas such as receptions should be easy to access from the entrance, while offices holding confidential information (such as legal, financial or HR data) should be more deeply embedded within your secure area and harder to reach from the perimeter. You may also want to actively distinguish the semi-public from the private areas by deploying a second secure perimeter.

12.3.2 Considerations for a second perimeter

Semi-public areas such as receptions, rooms used for interviews and warehouses are within your perimeter, but necessarily require a different approach from something such as a server room or secure area. To maintain accessibility while providing an adequate level of security for this second perimeter, consider visitor logs, security cameras and similar measures.

Be aware, however, of the risk malicious individuals may pose to semi-public (or even public) areas that you cannot 'police' as actively, such as car parks. Take the example discussed in 9.2 of an unmarked USB stick left in such a semi-public area – if an employee picks it up and plugs it into their computer to find out what is on it, they might inadvertently install malware or even irreparably destroy the hardware of the connected PC. Risks such as this can be mitigated by staff training and awareness programmes (see 12.11).

If you share your physical premises with another organisation, you almost certainly need more than one secure perimeter. For instance, the first perimeter may have a staffed reception desk that lets employees of both organisations onto the property according to jointly agreed procedures. The second perimeter would then be up to each organisation individually, which might restrict access to its own floors through, for example, a separate reception desk or key cards, with further security measures considered as described in the next few subsections and in 12.3.1.

If your employees make use of shared workspaces, it is wise to consider them a public area (since you have a much weaker idea of who might enter them, and have little to no control over the physical security), and therefore treat any portable devices, paperwork, etc. used within them as assets outside your perimeter. These are discussed in more detail in 12.3.5.

12.3.3 Clear screen and clear desk policies

Having defined your physical perimeter and determined how you will secure it to stop unauthorised individuals gaining entry is a very good start, but in itself is not enough to consider yourself physically secure. Information leakage – where sensitive information is inadvertently accessible to unauthorised individuals (whether intruders or staff not authorised to view that information) – is another common physical threat.

This risk can be significantly reduced by implementing clear screen and clear desk policies. The idea for both is that employees do not leave sensitive information in plain view, but you do need a sensible, pragmatic approach to get the best results: leave sensitive paperwork in lockable drawers or filing cabinets when not in use, lock computers when away from the screen for any extended period of time and switch computers off and erase confidential information from whiteboards overnight. A more comprehensive policy might also state that where lockable cabinets or drawers are not available, those offices need to be locked if unoccupied, and that hard-copy documents should be scanned where possible, with the original either securely destroyed or locked away as a backup.

Having said that, clear screen and clear desk policies will not protect you when computers are in use and paperwork is left lying on desks, and someone from the outside (or from an adjacent building) uses a good zoom lens. You could even be vulnerable to an authorised visitor being shown around or on-site contractors. Thoroughly vetting third parties before letting them into the building will help, as will sending an all-staff email to alert them to the hours they should avoid leaving sensitive information in view. To protect yourself from people outside the building looking in, you could use one-way mirror film over windows or privacy screens on computers and laptops.

12.3.4 Secure information disposal

Another major cause of information leakage is inadequate secure disposal, for example, failing to securely erase hard drives or shred sensitive paperwork before disposal. Even something as seemingly trivial as not collecting printouts can reveal restricted information, either to staff who are not supposed to have access to that data or to on-site contractors such as cleaners or a maintenance crew. A 2019 Shred-it® report found that 65% of respondents were concerned about left-behind printouts that could lead to a data breach, and 71% have picked up or seen a confidential or sensitive document they found in a public space.[45] Only 45% of respondents shred documents in every office area, and 46% train employees about secure disposal.

Depending on your requirements, you may find it beneficial to use a certified third-party secure disposal service. It will likely prove more secure and convenient than in-house shredding, particularly if you have a lot of paperwork to securely destroy. For the same reason, outsourcing may also prove more economical than in-house shredding, particularly in the long-term.

However, even if you regularly use a certified secure disposal service, you should train all staff to recognise what constitutes confidential or sensitive information, be aware of its value and to appreciate that they need to take extra steps to protect such information, including secure storage and disposal. You should also have clear procedures in place for IT staff for securely discarding any IT equipment, including hard drives. That way, if there is a failure of process at the third party's end, your information remains secure (which is an example of defence in depth). It will also help stop confidential documents from ending up in the ordinary bin, which may then never be picked up by the disposal service to be securely destroyed.

Finally, archives, storage rooms and filing cabinets tend to get cluttered with piled-up paperwork. Scanning hard copies and then destroying them will help keep those areas manageable, but it may also be worth scheduling time every few months to go over the overflow and declutter the office,

---

[45] Shred-it®, "Security of Confidential Documents in the Workplace", September 2019, *https://www.shredit.com/en-us/resource-centre/white-papers-case-studies/security-of-confidential-documents-in-workplace*.

possibly with the help of your disposal service provider. This will not only help mitigate the risk of information leakage but also make it easier to find the papers you need, when you need them. The disposal timelines should be detailed in your data retention policy or schedule.

12.3.5 Assets outside your perimeter

The increasing popularity of flexible working and portable devices means that the number of assets outside of your perimeter is also growing. Whether making use of shared workspaces, working while commuting or in other public areas, or permitting working from home, any form of flexible or remote working introduces further security concerns and challenges that need to be addressed.

For portable devices, there are clear physical security concerns: these are not just comparatively easy to lose or have stolen, but also tend to hold significant amounts of confidential or sensitive data. Laptops can be physically locked down with a security cable, and further protected with a privacy filter or screen to make it harder for someone sitting next to you to look at your screen and potentially see confidential information.

You probably also need to encrypt all portable devices – including laptops, phones, tablets and removable media – to protect them from data exfiltration if they are lost or stolen (also see 12.7). However, even if the contents are encrypted, loss or theft of the device still amounts to losing the data on it, which could be disastrous if it has not been backed up elsewhere. Even if it has been backed up, it will take time and effort to restore that data, so preventing the loss or theft in the first place is infinitely preferable. Increasing staff vigilance through training to reinforce key concepts is a good idea (also see 12.11). You should also enforce a mobile device policy with explicit requirements for the use of mobile devices: do not leave devices visibly unattended (such as in the back seat of a car), always store them in a secure location (such as a hotel safe), etc.

You should also be clear, in an appropriate policy, about whether staff are permitted to bring or use their own devices. If they are, a dedicated BYOD policy is necessary to mitigate some of the risks personal devices may introduce, since your IT team will have considerably less control over them than company-provided devices. A BYOD policy should be clear about devices' access controls, how data may be downloaded and stored, and necessary actions in the event of a known or suspected compromise, including if the device is lost or stolen. You can also raise these points in staff training.

Policies and training should also cover matters such as taking paperwork home: staff should avoid taking confidential documents home, but if they remove them from the security of the office anyway, they should do so in an envelope that does not reveal its contents or, even better, a locked case, and should only be taken out in an area where someone cannot read over their shoulder. Confidential conversations should receive the same treatment: not in a public area. Where shared workspaces are used, a private room should be sought, which are often provided in the same building.

12.3.6 Cloud security

If you make use of the Cloud, you should consider any information stored on it as assets outside your perimeter, since the physical infrastructure on which your information is stored is controlled by the Cloud service provider. It is also extremely unlikely that you would be granted permission to physically audit that infrastructure. Nonetheless, it is important that you conduct some due diligence checks in light of the legal obligations you likely have: for instance, if you store PII in the Cloud, the Cloud provider will be deemed the 'processor' or 'service provider', with you as the 'controller' or 'business' under the GDPR and CPRA respectively.[46] The implications of this are that your organisation is responsible for the security of that data, and will be held accountable in the case of a breach at the Cloud provider's end.

There are several things you can check for to gain assurance on the security of the provider's physical infrastructure. For instance, many providers publicly offer details of their physical and operational security controls and processes. Cloud providers may also have received a relevant certification such as ISO 27001, which indicates that an authorised body external to the Cloud provider has independently verified that the security measures in place are properly implemented and fit for purpose. Other precautions you can take include carefully reviewing your contractual agreement with the Cloud provider for guarantees of adequate security (third-party contract reviews are discussed in more detail in 12.13.2).

At the end of the day, however, it is worth remembering that Cloud service providers have a vested interest in keeping their infrastructure secure, particularly if your contract stipulates security requirements that they must meet. This does not mean that you should take Cloud security for granted, but be aware that Cloud-related breaches are more

[46] Note that these are not the only data protection laws that set out such concepts and accompanying requirements.

likely to occur as the result of a customer error, such as not changing default passwords (see 12.6) or using inadequate access controls (see 12.4), rather than weak infrastructure on the service provider's side. As such, taking your own steps and precautions that are fully within your control can go a long way.

A relatively common issue, for instance, are automated backups to a Cloud service that has not been properly secured with appropriate access controls (this is a particularly big issue for BYOD users). With automated tools, criminals can and do search the Internet for such files in the Cloud that contain confidential data and download them. You might say that the door was left open, not even requiring a crowbar or battering ram to reach the assets behind it. (As an aside, should this happen to you, be sure to consider it a data breach.[47])

12.3.7 Environmental security

Unfortunately, the intruder and other human threats are not the only physical dangers to information security, although they are the primary ones that may affect confidentiality.

---

[47] Virgin Media had been disclosing unsecured PII for ten months, which was accessed by at least one unauthorised user. It publicly responded with "No, this was not a cyber-attack. […] No, our database was not hacked. […] Certain sources are referring to this as a data breach. The precise situation is that information stored on one of our databases has been accessed without permission. The incident did not occur due to a hack but as a result of the database being incorrectly configured". References: BBC News, "Virgin Media data breach affects 900,000 people", March 2020, *https://www.bbc.co.uk/news/business-51760510*; Virgin Media, "Virgin Media's data incident – Help and Advice", accessed July 2020, *https://www.virginmedia.com/help/data-incident/important-information*.

Even after establishing and securing your perimeter, your physical defences may be bypassed by another type of physical danger: the environmental threat. Whether natural or a man-made disaster, either can affect the integrity and especially availability of your information assets and processing activities.

Exactly what kind of environmental threats you should be prepared for entirely depend on your location and your business. Even if your organisation does not conduct laboratory or manufacturing work, your risk assessment (also see 12.12) should consider neighbouring businesses, since they may introduce risks that could impact you and/or your employees if they are, for example, an oil or pharmaceutical company that may attract protestors, vandals, arsonists, etc. Equally, your risk assessment should consider what sort of natural disasters or extreme weather conditions have been known to affect your area, how likely they are to occur and how you can prepare for them by putting appropriate defences in place, such as fire extinguishers and exits, and barriers to defend against flooding.

However, you should only put preventive measures in place where it is both feasible and cost-effective. Unfortunately, in a world where climate change is increasingly evident, you cannot prepare for unforeseen extreme weather conditions or natural disaster. On top of that, you cannot control neighbouring businesses' activities. You should therefore assume the worst, and plan how to continue your core business activities despite any disruptions.

This means having some business continuity plans in place that go beyond insurance – being able to file a claim will give you piece of mind, and is unquestionably an arrangement you should make, but it will not help you to continue delivering your service and offering customer support. Having your website down even for just a few minutes can drive customers and prospects away, so being ready to continue at least your core business processes even when disaster strikes can prove critical.

Contingency planning will vary widely per organisation, but could include actions as low-cost as storing backups in the Cloud, encouraging flexible working and spreading assets across multiple buildings. More comprehensive plans will also be clear about with whom responsibilities lie and who is responsible in their absence, contain call trees, specify recovery time objectives and detail step-by-step procedures for specific scenarios.

See 14.3 for a more comprehensive discussion on business continuity.

12.4 Identity and access control

> Measures to ensure that the person attempting to access information and information systems (physically or logically) is who they say they are and that they are authorised to access that information.
>
> **Key output:** Effective controls and policies that help verify the identity of users, prevent the misuse of privileged access rights and stop unauthorised individuals from entering the premises.

Identity and access controls, backed by appropriate policies, help organisations authenticate and authorise users, and ensure staff, contractors and systems can access only the information they are permitted to. Such controls should cover identification, authentication, authorisation and accountability (IAAA):

- **Identification:**
  Identifying someone by, for example, name, username or ID number.
- **Authentication:**
  Proving that they are who they say they are by, for example, entering a password or PIN number.
- **Authorisation:**
  Granting that person access to systems and data based on the two security principles discussed below.
- **Accountability:**
  Tracing individual account activities, and ensuring non-repudiation – in other words, being able to prove which actions were performed by what accounts.

Regarding authorisation, as tempting as it may be to opt for convenience by giving everyone access to everything, that kind of approach dramatically – and unnecessarily – increases the likelihood and severity of a compromise. To mitigate the risks, there are two key security principles to follow:

1. **The 'need to know' principle:**
   Granting users access to only the information required to perform their role effectively – for instance, only HR and finance staff need access to HR and financial data, and only some finance staff will need access to payroll information.

2. **The principle of least privilege (also referred to as 'PoLP' or 'principle of minimal privilege'):** Granting users only the privileges necessary to perform their role effectively – for instance, normal users do not need to install software, but may have to run backups; alternatively, certain users may need access to specific information without requiring editing rights.

These principles apply to both identity controls (which verify who the user/individual is) and access controls (which limit that person's access to the bare minimum necessary). The controls must also account for both physical and logical access to information and information systems.

For physical access, this might mean that you implement a card reader that identifies and authenticates card holders – who have been issued cards that only give them access to the areas they need access to – with a log automatically generated that covers both successful and failed attempts to enter the premises, which is regularly reviewed for abnormal or suspicious behaviour.

For logical access, this usually means each person has at least one individual user account, which can be accessed with a token such as their biometric data or a password (to name just two possible controls), and that account only grants them access to the information they need.

Remember that for both types of access, there will be individuals or users who have more privileges than others, usually called administrators. These persons in particular will need to be uniquely identified, and should have to meet tougher security requirements before they can make use of those extra access rights. This might imply, for instance, having to authenticate in at least two different ways (also see

12.4.2), or having stronger password requirements. Also make sure that individuals with administrator accounts also have a 'normal' user account, and that they only use their more privileged account when they actually need the administrator privileges.

A key benefit of linking identity to access is that you know who has access to what information or infrastructure. Using automated access logs will allow you to identify who has actually made use of that access (accountability), as well as any unusual behaviour that may signify a compromise (see 12.4.7). This means that each account should be linked to only one user so that any access (or access attempts) can be linked to a specific person – shared accounts that could be used by a number of people make this a significantly harder task.

12.4.1 The security principles and documentation

Both the 'need to know' and 'least privilege' principles should be incorporated in clearly documented procedures for creating new user accounts and regularly reviewing any special access privileges granted. You also need a documented procedure for people who change roles within the company to make sure their access rights are still appropriate, as well as a procedure for leavers, whose access rights and accounts should be removed or disabled. Also remember to consider the implications of accessing confidential information remotely and BYOD (if applicable).

Although effective policies and procedures should enforce both principles, it is also a good idea to create an organisational culture where staff recognise that different access levels serve different purposes. By extension, you can encourage them to think about whether they really need all the information they have access to and, where appropriate, initiate their own requests for unnecessary user rights to be removed or revoked.

12.4.2 Authentication factors

Fundamentally, identity control is about being able to validate who a person is; 'authentication factors' are the attributes by which you do so. For both physical and logical controls, there are three possible factors for authentication:

1. **'What you know'** – e.g. a password, passcode or PIN number.
2. **'What you have'** – e.g. a mobile phone (to send a one-time password (OTP) to[48]) or a key card.
3. **'What you are'** – e.g. a fingerprint (for biometric access controls).

In many cases, relying on just one of these classes (i.e. relying on single-factor authentication) is sufficient – again, cyber and information security is all about balancing risks against controls.

However, where you need to protect particularly high-value or sensitive information, such as access to a password manager or financial information, it is worth implementing a second (two-factor authentication or 2FA) and possibly even a third (multifactor authentication or MFA) authentication factor. Any additional factors should not rely on and should be different from the first factor to optimise

---

[48] OTPs are randomly generated one-use codes or passwords that expire after a set amount of time.

the security benefits. Make sure to not go overboard with extra authentication factors though, or things might become unnecessarily expensive and inefficient.

12.4.3 Logical access controls

Logical access controls, used to authenticate and authorise users to digital information and information systems, are the most common type of access control for cyber security purposes – most organisations use passwords in some shape or form; likewise, access management systems such as Active Directory (AD) are also very commonly used.

There are a range of logical controls you can rely on, including firewalls (see 12.5.5 and 12.9.3), encryption (see 12.7), network segmentation (see 12.9.2) and a network access control solution (which checks company and personal devices patch levels, security policy settings, etc., before allowing access to company resources), but one of the most commonly used – and misused – controls is passwords.

Note that it is entirely possible that alternative authentication methods such as biometric or hardware solutions will become the norm in the years to come – Bill Gates declared in as early as 2004 that passwords "just don't meet the challenge for anything you really want to secure"[49] – but, for now, passwords are the default method of authentication for a range of services. Moreover, things such as MFA and password managers are more common now than they were a decade ago, making passwords not just an easy-to-implement and low-cost option, but potentially also a fairly

---

[49] Munir Kotadia, "Gates predicts death of the password", *CNET*, February 2004, https://www.cnet.com/news/gates-predicts-death-of-the-password/.

secure one – provided that you apply them in appropriate areas (e.g. access to online accounts or guest Wi-Fi) and implement an effective password policy.

12.4.4 Password policy

Despite the fact that the number and size of data breaches has been more widely publicised in recent years, many users continue to have terrible password habits when left to their own devices – SplashData's most commonly hacked password lists, published annually from 2014–2019, has '123456' ranking at the top for six consecutive years.[50] In 2019, this was followed by '123456789', 'qwerty', 'password' and '1234567'.

The cyber security community will undoubtedly continue to make efforts to get people to use better passwords both at home and in the workplace. Meanwhile, organisations are best off relying on an effective password policy that balances strong passwords with practical considerations.

The most reliable way of enforcing password policies – and ensuring unique, strong passwords are used – is to minimise the burden on users, relying instead on technical measures as much as possible. The second key point is to encourage passwords that are easy for users to remember, but difficult for computers or individuals to guess – in other words, focus on length over complexity. As the NCSC points out, if you force users to come up with 'complex' passwords that are difficult to memorise, they will inevitably develop other bad

[50] TeamsID, "The Top 50 Worst Passwords of 2019", December 2019, *https://www.teamsid.com/1-50-worst-passwords-2019/*.

password habits, including predictable patterns.[51] Those can include:

- Replacing 'o' with '0', 'i' with '1', etc.;
- Consecutive numbers, often added to the end of a dictionary word;
- Repeated characters; and/or
- Easy keyboard patterns (e.g. 'qwerty').

Users are also more likely to opt for a shorter password, making it even easier to crack, and use the same (or a very similar) password for different accounts, making the possible impact of a breach much higher. If they use the same passwords for work and personal accounts, the risk is even further increased.

An alternative is to simply stipulate a minimum length, without stipulating any other requirements. This will encourage techniques such as putting three or four random words together, such as 'shelfpictureswimming' or 'mixertablehorseliquid' (also referred to as 'passphrases'). As long as the chosen words are not too obvious, such as sports teams or 'thisismyworkpassword', this can be an extremely secure way of coming up with passwords – after all, the number of possible combinations grows exponentially with each letter or character added – while helping users come up with good passwords that are easy for them to remember and difficult for computers to crack.

---

[51] NCSC, "Password administration for system owners – Password policy: updating your approach", November 2018, *https://www.ncsc.gov.uk/collection/passwords/updating-your-approach*.

Additionally, as the NCSC points out, complexity requirements will not protect your organisation from social engineering attacks or insecure password storage – having said that, any other kind of password requirements – including none at all – would have the same problems. It is therefore worth considering mandatory staff awareness training, conducted at inductions and repeated annually for all employees (we will discuss this in more depth in 12.11).

12.4.5 Keeping passwords secure

Setting strong passwords is just one element of good password management – storing them securely is just as important. A notorious example is that of TV5Monde: this French television network, which broadcasts internationally, filmed a piece on its premises while social media passwords were visible in the background.[52] (This has also happened to other organisations.)

Of course, this is a fairly extreme situation, but the simple fact that the password had been written down is bad security practice in itself. You should teach staff to not write passwords down anywhere or save them in an unencrypted document, and to never share their password with anyone. Additionally, if they suspect their account may have been compromised, ensure employees know that they need to report the incident to IT and change their password.

---

[52] BBC News, "France TV5Monde passwords seen on cyber-attack TV report", April 2015, *https://www.bbc.co.uk/news/world-europe-32248779*.

The above are only the basics when it comes to password security. There are many other ways in which passwords can be leaked or discovered, including via:

- Shoulder surfing (being seen typing in a password);
- A keylogger, intercepting any passwords typed in;
- Social engineering attacks (including phishing and coercion), trying to trick users into revealing their password;
- Brute-force attacks (guessing passwords through an automated process until the right one is found);
- Attackers attempting passwords from previously successful hacks (which targets people who reuse passwords but can particularly be a problem if staff tend to use common passwords); and
- Interception of passwords or password hashes as they are transmitted over a network.

A critical point to remember is that attackers do not need to be technically skilled to successfully intercept or determine someone's password, particularly as many automated tools are easily available online.

Fortunately, when it comes to keeping passwords secure, not everything relies on users' vigilance – your organisation's IT team should be able to implement certain technical measures, or at least advise on what third-party products offer enough security. To protect passwords at rest, make sure they are stored in a hashed (and ideally salted) format and never as plaintext. For passwords in transit, make sure that web applications use HTTPS if they require authentication. Finally, ensure the access management system itself is adequately protected (you may need to get in touch with third-party suppliers to check this).

12.4.6 Password managers

Password managers (or password vaults) can solve the problem of remembering lots of complicated passwords for both work and at home, and may even have a feature that automatically generates complex, unique passwords for every account. These features generate extremely strong and complex passwords – the kind a human probably cannot remember – while also removing nearly all password burdens from the user, as they will only have to devise and memorise one set of hard-to-guess login credentials for the password manager itself.

Of course, this is not a perfect solution, if only because there is a chance of having all your accounts breached at once. However, that chance is *extremely* small for host-based password managers, as an attacker would need your master password as well as access to your machine or device.[53] Password managers are inherently designed to be secure, but as an additional security measure (and for peace of mind), you might like to consider a second authentication factor. That way, in the event your master password is breached, an intruder should not be able to access your plaintext passwords.

Remember that good security is not about being impenetrable – it is about mitigating and minimising the risks. And, as the NCSC points out, a password manager is a

---

[53] Password managers that synchronise with an online database should only keep a salted hash of the master password, and have a vested interest in protecting your information.

good, secure option, provided that you deploy it correctly.[54] That means:

- Only use a trustworthy software provider;
- Enable 2FA/MFA; and
- Ensure (through your password policy and technical controls) that users choose a strong master password and keep it secure.

12.4.7 Technical controls for passwords

There are other technical controls you can and should employ to enforce or strengthen your password policy, thereby generally improving your security.

Single sign-on (SSO)

You can strengthen your overall security by implementing SSO, which will allow staff to get access to all or a subset of their accounts after authenticating just once. The idea is that by making it easier for users to log on, people are more likely to choose a strong password if they do not need to repeatedly retype it or memorise multiple passwords.

However, this does come with some risk: if a user's account is compromised, the attacker will have access to all their accounts. To reduce that risk, limit the accounts that can be accessed via SSO, or consider implementing MFA.

---

[54] NCSC, "What does the NCSC think of password managers?", January 2017, *https://www.ncsc.gov.uk/blog-post/what-does-ncsc-think-password-managers*.

Password blacklisting

Both the NCSC[55] and the National Institute of Standards and Technology (NIST)[56] recommend using a password blacklist to mitigate the risk of users choosing a password that meets complexity or length requirements but is nonetheless easy to guess (such as 'Password123!'). Such a list typically consists of passwords that have repeatedly been hacked in the past (which are published online and shared among criminal hackers), but users have also been known to tailor it their organisation.

The NCSC has released a file that contains 100,000 commonly hacked passwords, and believes it to be a good number as it feels it achieves "a [good] balance between protecting users from making poor password choices, whilst not making it too difficult for them to choose one".[57] You can also opt for a third-party password blacklisting service to make sure your list stays up to date.

Password expiry

Regularly changing passwords prevents indefinite access in case of an undiscovered compromise, but is nonetheless far from a perfect solution. For one, a password reset will not

---

[55] NCSC, "Passwords, passwords everywhere – How password blacklists can help your users to make sensible password choices", April 2019, *https://www.ncsc.gov.uk/blog-post/passwords-passwords-everywhere*.

[56] NIST, "NIST Special Publication 800-63B – Digital Identity Guidelines", June 2017, *https://pages.nist.gov/800-63-3/sp800-63b.html*.

[57] "Passwords, passwords everywhere – How password blacklists can help your users to make sensible password choices."

tell you whether a compromise has occurred, and relying on periodic password changes may give a potential attacker weeks or even months of access to a compromised account. Moreover, if the compromise was caused by insecure storage of passwords, the attacker can likely locate the new password with relative ease (and if they have access to the breached account, they will probably be aware of the password expiry notification).

On top of that, there is a risk of user forgetfulness, which can lead to a loss in productivity as users regularly contact the helpdesk or, worse, lead to passwords being written down. Alternatively, they may be inclined to pick a new password similar to the old one.

For the above reasons, the NCSC recommends only forcing password changes in the event of a known or suspected compromise,[58] although periodic password changes may be valuable for accounts with privileged access rights. You should also change the password of a shared account if someone does not need (or is not permitted) to access it anymore.

However, before you can forego periodic password changes for all accounts, you need to be confident in your ability to identify a possible breach. It will certainly help if you encourage staff to report any suspicious activity, and being quick about disabling or removing unnecessary accounts mitigates the risk of a compromise in the first place. There are, however, other measures that can help detect and

---

[58] "Password administration for system owners – Password policy: updating your approach."

prevent intrusions, including security monitoring and account lockouts.

Security monitoring and account lockouts

Each login or login attempt should generate a record in an access log, showing unique identifiers for each attempted login. By regularly reviewing access logs, you may be able to pinpoint abnormal or suspicious behaviour. Automated tools can assist this process, although human intervention will be required to determine whether it really was a breach of security.

Suspicious behaviour could include:

- Login attempts at unexpected times or from unexpected geographical areas;
- Password spraying (attempting the same small number of passwords on a large number of accounts);
- Login attempts where only the first step of MFA was successful; and
- A large number of failed login attempts (such as five to ten attempts within a short space of time).

The automated response to these behaviours should be account lockouts or 'throttling' (progressively increasing the waiting time between successive login attempts), as this could be the sign of a brute-force attack. However, remember that this could also just be a legitimate user forgetting their password, so make sure there is a way for legitimate users to recover their password and unlock the device.

For a more in-depth discussion on security monitoring, see 13.2.

12.4.8 Physical access controls

Although logical access controls, especially passwords, are more commonly used in a cyber security context than physical controls, it is important to not forget about the latter. As discussed in 12.3, information security is not just about protecting yourself from attacks conducted over the Internet, but also about not allowing unauthorised individuals onto the premises. This involves, among other things, ensuring that sites are locked up outside office hours, contractors are properly vetted, staff challenge strangers on site, and tailgating and piggybacking are prevented.[59] You may also want to implement controls that identify the specific person and can be recorded (i.e. incorporate identity control).

There are a number of controls you could use to achieve this – a few of them below are listed below, along with some of the risks for each. Note that not all of them may apply, depending on the exact implementation of that control.

Key and lock

A simple but effective way of controlling access. Although a relatively primitive form of access control, it still works and, in a business setting, is very suitable for private offices or offices shared by very few people, and for filing cabinets and drawers.

Risks: Lost, stolen or forgotten keys; forgetting to lock the door/cabinet/drawer; leaving the key in the lock.

---

[59] With piggybacking, a person tags along with another, authorised person. With tailgating, an unauthorised individual follows an authorised person into a secure area without consent.

Combination lock or PIN pad

A mechanical (combination lock) or digital (PIN pad) lock that requires a number combination to open. As physical keys do not need to be issued, it is a more practical access control for areas or cabinets with many authorised users.

Risks: Someone overseeing the number combination (both) or working it out based on fingerprints/numbers wearing away (PIN pad); forgetting or writing down the code (both); failing to mix up digits properly (combination lock).

Card reader

A device that grants access via access or ID cards. If worn visibly (e.g. around employees' necks), it has the added benefit of being able to tell whether someone is authorised to be there. These cards can be linked to the user's access rights so the card reader is able to permit or deny access appropriately.

Risks: Lost, stolen or forgotten cards; staff wearing their ID card outside the building.

Biometric access control points

Devices that can recognise a part of your body, such as a fingerprint, palm or eye, to grant access or unlock something. Has the benefit of not having to issue physical keys of any kind, and mitigates the risk of people forgetting or (inadvertently) sharing any codes. Can also be used to positively identify the specific person who uses the lock.

Risks: Personal data risks (particularly as biometric data is usually considered sensitive/special category data under modern data protection law, and requires extra protection); does not work for everyone (e.g. because of scarring or skin conditions) and/or can present hygiene problems.

Security guards and CCTV

One or more employees who safeguard the physical perimeter, possibly by watching the live CCTV footage. They may also be responsible for checking and verifying the credentials of anyone wishing to enter the premises. Having visible CCTV cameras may also act as a preventive and/or forensic measure, but remember that you may need to put up a public CCTV notice to meet your data protection obligations.

Risks: Human error; cameras being covered up or out of order; overwritten recordings; not meeting data protection obligations or cameras picking up excessive data (e.g. passer-byers' faces).

Man traps/airlocks

A small space with two sets of doors that people have to walk through to access a secure perimeter (particularly high-security areas). The first door has to fully close before the second one opens, and a second set of credentials may be required to get through the second door. Used to prevent tailgating, and could be used to check a person's weight to ensure that equipment is not being brought in or taken out, or to contain an intruder.

Risks: Trapping someone; reduction in productivity.

Each control has its own benefits and drawbacks (as well as its own risks), so it is extremely likely you will need to use a mix of them to cover different areas of the business effectively. The non-exhaustive list above, for instance, includes controls that differ in scalability, cost, level of security and key or card management requirements (many of which are correlated, positively or negatively).

12.5 Malware protection

Measures that protect your computer systems and information from a broad range of malware.

Key output: Technical and organisational measures, including anti-malware software and an anti-malware policy, which protect your organisation from malware.

Malware is one of the most common technical threats that can cause significant damage; for example, global aluminium supplier Norsk Hydro suffered a ransomware attack that cost an estimated 550–650 million NOK (about £46–55 million or $59–70 million).[60] Fortunately, fairly basic controls are already sufficient to mitigate the vast majority of malware attacks, with managing all data import and export – in other words, scanning all data at your network perimeters – key to keeping malware out.

We will discuss a number of defence options below. For a more detailed discussion on malware types, see 7.2.

---

[60] Norsk Hydro, "Cyber-attack on Hydro", November 2019, *https://www.hydro.com/en/media/on-the-agenda/cyber-attack/*.

12.5.1 Anti-malware policy

A good starting point is an anti-malware policy, which should make your organisation's position on protecting itself from malware clear, and set out rules such as complying with software licence agreements, forbidding the use of unauthorised software and establishing how removable media is handled. The policy could also make breaking certain rules a disciplinary offence.

The exact contents of the policy will depend on your organisation's circumstances and requirements. It is therefore best if you draft it on the basis of a risk assessment, or adjust it in line with the result of an assessment conducted at a later stage. You should also regularly review it to account for the latest technical advice, such as that published by the NCSC, NIST or Virus Bulletin (see 13.1 for more on threat and vulnerability intelligence).

Also remember that many viruses and other malware are introduced accidentally. This might be because an employee inserted a USB stick already infected (without being aware of it), or mistakenly clicked on a malicious link or downloaded a malicious file. A strong anti-malware policy, enforced by technical controls and staff training, can prevent many such incidents.

12.5.2 Raise awareness

Although technical controls play an essential part in stopping malware from getting onto your networks, staff awareness is just as critical, from appreciating that security is everyone's responsibility to knowing how to help prevent malware infections from occurring. As mentioned before, many infections happen accidentally as the result of an employee's actions. Training and awareness help staff recognise threats and take appropriate action, as well as appreciate what role they play in protecting the organisation.

Your training can cover topics such as:

- The risks of malware;
- Different types of malware and their characteristics;
- How to prevent – and recognise – malware infections;
- What to do if you think you may have clicked a malicious link or installed malicious software; and
- The possible impact, financial or otherwise, of a malware infection, including real-life examples.

We will discuss staff awareness and training in more depth in 12.11.

12.5.3 Antivirus and anti-malware software

Antivirus and anti-malware software are some of the most common anti-malware measures, and are often included for free in popular operating systems, including Windows (Defender) and macOS (XProtect), supporting the 'secure by design' approach encouraged by the UK government (also see 12.8).[61] Simply enabling them can make you significantly more secure, but you will need to keep them up to date to make sure they remain effective against the latest threats (more on patch management in 12.5.9 and 12.6).

Besides enabling and keeping your anti-malware software up to date, you also have to run regular, full scans. These can be set to run automatically, for example, every day or every week at a certain time, but you can also do this on a per-

[61] UK Department for Digital, Culture, Media & Sport, "Secure by Design", June 2019, *https://www.gov.uk/government/collections/secure-by-design*.

access basis, such as when removable media like a USB stick is plugged in, or when an email attachment is being downloaded – in other words, at the points where malware may enter your network.

Although many free anti-malware measures are sufficient for a large number of users, particularly those new to cyber security and/or when paired with techniques such as whitelisting, you may want to look into enterprise anti-malware options as your network grows and cyber security maturity improves (depending on your needs, of course). Enterprise solutions will offer better support in the event of an infection and are typically better able to manage threats that are unique to business environments and complex networks. Larger packages will also include other network controls to support network segregation, boundary protection, etc.

12.5.4 Mobile anti-malware software

Although less well known, antivirus and anti-malware software solutions also exist for smartphones and tablets. Consider how attractive company devices can be as malware targets – they often store or have access to significant amounts of confidential or sensitive information, but also often lack the security computers tend to have.

Risk management is key here: if staff mobile devices can access particularly valuable or a lot of information, it is probably worth installing and maintaining some kind of anti-malware software. If they cannot access or store that kind of information, only allowing users to download from official app stores may already be sufficient to reduce the risk of mobile malware (since users will benefit from the security checks those stores conduct on the apps they list, and the fact that the app stores can remove apps from users' devices if they pass the initial checks but prove potentially harmful at a later date).

The risk can be further reduced by also whitelisting apps – in other words, only allowing certain approved apps to be installed (discussed in more detail in 12.5.6). Since code signing is now common on modern devices, which will confirm the identity of the developer and that the code has not been altered or otherwise tampered with since it was signed off, you can enforce whitelisting fairly reliably. Discouraging or preventing users from connecting to public or untrusted Wi-Fi points, instead relying on mobile data, will also help mitigate the risk of mobile malware infections.

Of course, combining all four measures – mobile anti-malware software, restricting app downloads to official app stores only, app whitelisting and not connecting to untrusted Wi-Fi points – is the most secure option, but also requires more resources and can be disruptive to users. Ultimately, you have to decide how big the risk is, and what controls are sufficient to bring that risk down to an acceptable level.

12.5.5 Firewalls

Firewalls provide a barrier to traffic seeking to cross the perimeter by only allowing authorised traffic to pass – this requires setting the default firewall rule to 'deny' and enforcing a whitelist with authorised protocols, ports and applications. Effectively, firewalls work as a filter that protects your boundaries, and host-based firewalls are particularly important when using public or untrusted Wi-Fi networks. They are usually a first port of call for organisations looking to secure their network perimeters, since systems will be better protected against potentially malicious traffic.

Much like anti-malware or antivirus software, it is now common for operating systems to offer a firewall service as standard (including Windows Defender Firewall), so simply enabling it may already be sufficient for your needs. If you require a more sophisticated approach, many other firewalls are still available on the market, but it is important to make sure that your anti-malware software can work together with that firewall.

Firewalls are discussed in more depth in 12.9.

12.5.6 Whitelisting

Whitelisting involves creating a list of permitted applications on a device, and blocking any application (or processes within a certain application) not appearing on that list from running. Essentially, it treats everything as a potential threat to stop users installing and running unauthorised, and possibly infected, applications.

It is a useful technique, particularly in combination with anti-malware software, since it mitigates the risk of the software not detecting some malware, and works both for computers and mobile devices (see 12.5.3 and 12.5.4). However, it can increase administrator workload if it is especially restrictive, or impact user productivity if deployed poorly, so it is important to strike the right balance between usability and security.

Another benefit of whitelisting is that it requires significantly less maintenance than software, since it does not rely as strongly on keeping up to date with the latest threats. However, the list may still need to be reviewed periodically and/or when users ask permission to download or run software not on the whitelist.

You can base your whitelist on several things, including executable names or paths, digital signatures, file or cryptographic hashes and regular expression (regex) matching. The actual process of compiling the whitelist also has multiple options. For smaller organisations, it may be feasible to compile your own, but you could also look into whitelisting services and software. These already have a list with known good executables and domains set up, which you can then tailor to your requirements. It is also becoming increasingly common to see anti-malware software, firewalls and application whitelisting offered as a bundle.

Of course, whitelisting may not be a convenient solution for everyone. For instance, it could overburden IT, or you may want to permit specific users only to download certain software. For the latter, whitelist software that allows an administrator to define some exceptions, permitting specific users to execute certain applications at specified times, might be a good solution.

12.5.7 Grey- and blacklisting

For email, greylisting may also be a good alternative to whitelisting, since spam detectors may accidentally filter out legitimate emails. By deploying greylisting for email, you can reject emails from unknown or suspicious senders on a temporary basis. The idea is that legitimate senders will try again later, whereas spammers tend to mass-email and will therefore not retry an address that already rejected them.

For preventing users from accessing malicious websites, whitelisting is not practical because it is virtually impossible to predict what websites users may require as part of everyday business. A better solution for safe surfing is to deploy blacklisting to block access to known malicious websites or websites with certain characteristics (for example, expired certificates or containing certain keywords). Although such a blacklist could never be completely secure, since the number of malicious websites is ever-growing, it can significantly mitigate the risk of a click to the wrong website, in error or otherwise, and downloading malware as a result.

You can also set up your blacklist to give a pop-up warning to users that are about to enter an unknown, and therefore potentially malicious, domain. You can then force them to return to the page they came from or let them confirm that they want to proceed to the unknown page.

12.5.8 Sandboxing

Sandboxing involves running an application in an isolated environment, limiting its access to the rest of your networks and devices. The idea is that sandboxing will prevent scenarios such as a USB stick containing malware (whether known or not) plugged into someone's computer infecting the rest of your network. Some browsers and similar software incorporate simple sandboxing features to protect users as they browse; you should confirm that your chosen application supports this before relying on it.

More traditional sandboxes are essentially small, segregated networks, and might exist solely on virtual machines. They often mimic an 'ordinary' network in terms of the operating systems, software and applications in place, which enables admins to see how a piece of software or suspected malware affects a known environment. In practical terms, this might involve scanning the content of any removable media before it can be inserted into someone's computer.

To further help prevent the infected USB scenario, you could:

- Encourage staff to share files via email, secure file sharing services and the Cloud instead of removable media;
- Provide company-issued removable media that staff may use within the organisation *only*; and
- Restrict access to physical ports.

12.5.9 Keep systems up to date

Manufacturers and developers normally release regular updates that not only improve your IT equipment or software but also patch known vulnerabilities, since these are what malware usually attempt to exploit and are natural targets for criminal hackers. Systems that are running older versions of software – or software that is no longer supported – are a common factor in many security breaches, so installing vendor updates as soon as they are available is vital to minimise the time frame in which a known vulnerability can be exploited.

Patch management is discussed in more depth in 12.6.

12.5.10 Secure backups

Taking regular backups is one of the most basic and oldest cyber security controls, but it is particularly important. In the event that malware breaks through your defences and infects your systems, having backups handy means, for instance, that ransomware cannot effectively force you to pay a ransom. (Of course, the actual process of restoring that data can be time-consuming, so it is far better to prevent the attack from occurring in the first place by having other measures in place.) In similar logic, you may also need to rebuild infected machines from a good image (see 12.6.1) that has been hardened.

Having said that, some ransomware variants can delete or infect your backups too (such as Zenis ransomware, which even overwrites your backups before it deletes them to ensure you absolutely cannot recover your data[62]), so make sure that the backup service itself is adequately protected by measures such as anti-malware software. Also remember that malware can remain dormant for long periods before triggering, so think about how frequently you need to run your backups and how long to retain them. This will completely depend on how critical the information is for you; for instance, if you rely on data coming in constantly, you probably need at least daily backups that may not need to be kept for more than a week.

You should also think about how you store your backups. You should restrict access in line with the two security principles discussed in 12.4 – 'need to know' and 'least privilege'. Since you want to minimise the risk of any account breach potentially leading to your backups being contaminated, or even a careless employee accidentally deleting them, make sure only users who might need to restore the data backed up can access them by implementing appropriate logical and physical access controls.

---

[62] New Jersey Cybersecurity & Communications Integration Cell (NJCCIC), "Zenis", March 2018, *https://www.cyber.nj.gov/threat-profiles/ransomware-variants/zenis*.

A final point to remember is that you probably keep some hard-copy data, which can be destroyed too, albeit not in a ransomware attack but as the result of a fire or flood (among other things). You could, for example, make it a policy to keep digital copies of important documentation or keep copies on different sites, but the best approach will vary per organisation, depending on the amount and importance of the paperwork. The key point is not to overlook hard-copy data, and make sure that you secure it and back it up.

12.6 Configuration and patch management

Software and IT equipment are securely configured and kept up to date, and retired where they are no longer supported.

Key output: A systematic process for minimising vulnerabilities affecting hardware and software through secure configurations and patching.

The default configurations on IT equipment and software are often as open as possible for maximum convenience, but this also provides more access points for unauthorised users, increasing your organisation's attack surface (the total sum of vulnerabilities). It is therefore a good idea to 'harden' your systems, which involves disabling or removing any unnecessary functions, and changing default passwords (see 12.4 for an in-depth discussion on passwords and other access controls) to reduce your attack surface and, by extension, the risk of a security breach. In the case of externally facing devices, unused ports should be closed.

However, just setting up and configuring your devices and software securely is not enough to stay protected – it is at least equally important to regularly update and patch them. Systems running older versions of software, or software that is no longer supported by the developer, are a common factor in many security breaches. According to the Bulletproof Annual Cyber Security Industry Report 2020, 50% of critical or high-level risks originate from outdated, unpatched or unsupported components.[63]

Out-of-date software is often subject to a number of vulnerabilities that later versions have addressed. Although the average user is unlikely to be aware of these vulnerabilities, well-informed attackers often seek to take advantage in the time frame between information about a vulnerability being made available and remediations being implemented (zero-day attacks). Generally speaking, there are three windows where a vulnerability is most likely to be exploited:

1. Before you have securely configured your device/software or identified the vulnerability.
2. Before the vendor has made a patch available.
3. Before every machine has installed that patch.

As soon as the details of a new vulnerability have been revealed, a means of exploiting it (such as malware) can appear in hours. With time so tight, having a preferably automated process that reliably updates your systems as soon

---

[63] Bulletproof, "Annual Cyber Security Industry Report 2020", January 2020, *https://www.bulletproof.co.uk/industry-reports/bulletproof-annual-cyber-security-report-2020*.

as the vendor releases a patch is critical (discussed further in 12.6.3).

If the vendor stops offering support altogether, you should replace or retire that device/software. If you are looking for a replacement, be sure to check how long the vendor intends to support it. After all, a slightly older version may seem cheaper, but it could prove to be a false economy if you need to find another replacement in a year's time – and more expensive still if you keep it and suffer a breach as a result.

The 2017 WannaCry attack is a particularly good example of this: the malware targeted a vulnerability in Windows that already had a patch available, but not for legacy versions of Windows such as XP (for which support stopped in 2014). Windows XP users, including parts of the UK's National Health Service (NHS), were among those affected by WannaCry, and the attack ended up costing the NHS alone £92 million (about $118 million).[64] WannaCry is also a good example of how quickly malware can spread: exact numbers vary per report, but it is certain that hundreds of thousands of computers were infected within one day. (The WannaCry case study is discussed in more detail in 8.4.)

12.6.1 Secure configuration

Poor system configurations could permit an external attacker or, for that matter, an unauthorised internal user, to access information or functions they are not meant to, making it possible, for instance, for a standard user account to in practice have elevated privileges. Not all vulnerabilities are necessarily 'dangerous' in themselves but can, for example,

---

[64] "Securing cyber resilience in health and care: October 2018 progress update."

give the attacker vital information about software version numbers or systems in use, which may tell them what vulnerabilities to attempt to exploit, or help them prepare a more sophisticated attack.

Hardening your systems involves, for example, disabling or removing any functions, accounts, etc. that you do not require, such as default guest accounts, as a standard part of installation. You could ensure this by detailing secure configuration procedures in your operational instructions, and recording system configuration changes in your event logs (see 12.4.7).

You can also make use of 'images' to make life easier, which are a complete snapshot of a device's settings and software, usually stored as a 'golden' or 'master' image so that devices with similar needs can be set up to the same secure standard. These 'templates' let your IT department quickly set up a device without having to remember the same steps for disabling functions, removing accounts, etc., after which they can make changes according to the user's specific needs. Images also help you keep an eye on the overall configuration of the device without getting lost checking the settings of individual software or hardware elements.

You should also regularly review the systems and software you have in place as part of a change management process – needs change over time, and where a particular software is no longer required, you should remove it. Doing so reduces the number of access points and potential 'back doors', which will help mitigate the risk of a security breach, accidental or otherwise. Equally, by anticipating what changes need to be made and when, you also avoid service unavailability and errors caused by time pressure.

Finally, make sure to implement suitable access controls, change default passwords, and grant access on 'need to know' and 'least privilege' bases only – secure configuration and access controls go hand in hand (see 12.4 for a full discussion of access control). However, remember that being too restrictive can hinder users in doing their jobs and may increase the burden on the helpdesk, so be sure to balance security with usability.

12.6.2 Patching

Of course, secure configuration from the start is just one element of keeping your systems secure – another is regularly updating and patching them. This is a process that can be automated to reduce the burden on IT.

Patches usually include a set of changes that:

- Address vulnerabilities not identified when the software was first released, or vulnerabilities introduced by other patches or the interactivity between systems and/or applications;
- Fix software bugs; and/or
- Generally improve the software's functionality or performance.

The idea of patches is that relatively minor changes can be made to the software fairly efficiently, without having to tamper with the source code or reassemble the program. From a security perspective, the 'efficiently' part is essential – we have already discussed how fast a newly discovered vulnerability can be exploited, so quickly creating and installing a suitable patch can mitigate that risk.

Having said that, there are some negatives to bear in mind. Since developers are usually under significant pressure to release patches as soon as possible, particularly those that are meant to address security issues, there is a risk that the patch introduces undesired side effects or does not adequately mitigate the vulnerability.

To manage those risks, it is sensible to first test the patch in a sandboxed environment (also see 12.5.8). That way, you can check for any undesired effects, such as slowing down the system or changes to usability, before you install the patch across the estate. Reading the patch notes, which should detail what the patch does, can also often catch potential issues before deployment. Where the negative impact of a patch outweighs its benefits, you could choose to not apply or delay installing that patch. However, that decision needs to be made by someone with a thorough understanding of not just the risk but also the application and its use, and you need to be prepared to take alternative steps to mitigate the risk – for example, temporarily disabling the software.

If you are not able to adequately test the patch before installing it (for example, because of a lack of resources), you could consider delaying the patch until other users have reported their experiences. This must, however, be weighed against the risk of not patching promptly.

Whatever approach you take, ensure it is clearly laid out in a patching policy. This should set out your organisation's approach to patching, assert that no unsupported software will be used (or set out exceptions to that), how patches are assessed (if at all), deadlines for approved patches to be applied (which might vary depending on the type of software), etc. Policies and procedures as part of a formal information security management programme are discussed in more detail in 15.1.

12.6.3 Asset and vulnerability management

Earlier, we mentioned the need for a process that reliably updates your systems in response to the vendor releasing a patch – setting software to update automatically can go a long way to achieving that. However, you also need a way of ensuring that you have not missed any software. For that, an up-to-date asset inventory (also see 12.1) for your hardware and software is a prerequisite – this is why patch management software often also functions as an asset management tool. For vulnerability management purposes, your asset inventory should at least detail:

- Vendor name and contact details;
- Version numbers;
- Patch statuses and regime;
- Location; and
- Asset owners.

The necessity of an asset inventory for patch and vulnerability management is twofold. First, knowing what hardware and software has been authorised will help you identify any unauthorised items (you could deploy a tool to automate, or partially automate, this process). Second, a digital list of your assets can be linked to a vulnerability database, which will help you receive comprehensive information on technical vulnerabilities in a timely manner, and allow you to conduct vulnerability scans to validate your patching.

12.6.4 Validating your configurations and patching

It is important to validate both your configurations and patching, which can be done by regularly running an automated vulnerability scan, possibly supplemented with penetration testing. As an extra precaution, asset owners should also regularly check vendor notifications and the list of patches the vendor provides on its website (or delegate that responsibility) to make sure all patches have been installed correctly, particularly if they notice odd behaviour.

Vulnerability scanning and penetration testing are discussed in more detail in 13.1.2 and 13.1.3 respectively.

12.7 Encryption

> Cryptographic solutions, including encryption, pseudonymisation and anonymisation, are deployed where necessary to reduce the risk to information at rest and in transit. Encryption and decryption keys are kept secure.
>
> **Key output:** An encryption policy that makes clear when to use encryption and how keys are protected, and appropriate technical measures to enforce the policy.

Encryption, a common form of cryptography, is a means of protecting your confidential information when at rest, in transit or both. The idea is that a mathematical function encodes your data by using a secret value or 'key', ensuring that only authorised users and applications that hold the decryption key can view that information, thereby protecting its confidentiality and integrity. Encryption solutions are widely available, with many affordable options, but are not a 'silver bullet' solution.

For example, a website might offer an encrypted connection with the browser, which protects confidentiality and integrity in case of interception, by using HTTPS (as opposed to HTTP) and holding a valid SSL certificate. Clearly, that is a good thing, and is something staff should be trained to look out for (see 12.11). However, you should also make staff aware that it is possible for attackers to spoof the entire address bar, including the padlock icon (which indicates that HTTPS is in use), and that there is nothing stopping a malicious actor from securing an SSL certificate and offering an encrypted connection to their own website. In other words, encryption in this context does not automatically imply that the website is actually safe, but it is nonetheless something you should look out for, as any website you want to trust with your information should use HTTPS (for more on communications security, see 12.9).

As another example, encrypting portable devices is something you most certainly should do, since it will protect data if the device is lost or stolen. In other words, it will protect that data's confidentiality and integrity. Having said that, losing that device still amounts to data loss, affecting its availability, which can be disastrous if that data has not been backed up (and even then it will take time and effort to restore it). Again, encryption is a good measure that should be deployed, but it can only protect the confidentiality and integrity of information – not its availability, meaning that you will need to implement further measures to protect that aspect of security and develop a more resilient posture, such as taking backups.

In short, encryption is a valuable security measure that should be considered and to some extent deployed, but should also be used in combination with other security measures, including staff training (see 12.11) and backups. Encryption is also not the only valid solution for protecting your data – depending on the context, pseudonymisation and anonymisation may be good alternatives.

If you do deploy encryption, you should also consider at what stage(s) in the lifecycle to encrypt your information, and how you will protect your encryption and decryption keys.

12.7.1 Deciding whether and when to use encryption

Generally speaking, there are two main scenarios in which encryption should be considered: for information storage (at rest) and information transfers (in transit). In both cases, it can prevent unauthorised access and modification, but needs to be deployed and used correctly in order to be effective (and even then is not foolproof).

Importantly, the key needed to decrypt the information needs to remain secret, or the encryption is ineffective. Equally, if the key is lost, the availability of the information has been compromised, making it inaccessible even to authorised individuals. Keys can also be cracked as computers become more powerful, so the algorithm and keys should be subject to regular review and, if required, updated. Checking what authorities such as NIST say about specific encryption standards – which ones are deemed secure, which ones are cause for concern for certain applications and which ones are deemed obsolete – is generally a good place to look.

For example, the Data Encryption Standard (DES) was developed in the early 1970s and retired in 2005. Despite early criticism for its short key length (which is why it was eventually retired – it is no longer secure for most applications because of today's computational power available), DES was highly influential in advancing modern cryptography, with 3DES among its successors. In turn, the usage of 3DES was restricted by NIST in 2017, placing an upper limit of data that one single key bundle can encrypt, since it is no longer deemed secure for bigger quantities.[65]

When considering whether to use encryption, bear in mind that most processing activities require the information to be unencrypted on either end of a communication or when the processing activity is 'active', so encryption may not be a suitable protective measure for every activity.

Whether you should deploy encryption depends on a few factors:

- How likely is it that the information might be accessed and/or modified by an unauthorised individual?
- If the information is breached, how significant would the consequences be to your organisation and, if applicable, the individuals to whom the information relates? In other words, how sensitive or confidential is the information?
- Are there legal or contractual requirements to encrypt the data?

As for the likelihood of a breach, portable devices and removable media, for example, are relatively easy to lose or have stolen; additionally, portable devices may connect to insecure/public Wi-Fi. Removable media and, in particular, portable devices, are also likely to contain or have access to business-critical information. As such, the risk of unauthorised access or modification is very high, making it

---

[65] Elaine Barker and Nicky Mouha, "Recommendation for the Triple Data Encryption Algorithm (TDEA) Block Cipher", *Special Publication (NIST SP) – 800-67rev2*, November 2017, *https://www.nist.gov/publications/recommendation-triple-data-encryption-algorithm-tdea-block-cipher-1*.

wise to encrypt the information stored on them, on top of password-protecting them.

Two more examples are when you are emailing sensitive information or storing it in the Cloud. In either case, the impact of any breach can be significant, and encryption can be a good solution for mitigating that risk. In the case of the Cloud, it is probably better to encrypt data before transmitting it to the Cloud; however, you probably do not need to encrypt every email – just those that contain sensitive or confidential information. To help staff decide when to deploy encryption, a dedicated policy may help, in which you can stipulate points such as:

- Encrypting confidential or sensitive information such as PII, or sending it via a protected/encrypted service other than email, which might include:
    - Using a dedicated system for information transfers that is encrypted and/or access controlled;
    - Encrypting the information before attaching it to the email; or
    - Using a different, dedicated email account (not the user's normal email) to send that data.
- Always encrypting data on laptops, mobile devices and removable media, and password-protecting the devices where possible; and
- Always encrypting authentication credentials (e.g. passwords) and other authentication information both at rest and in transit. Nobody, including your IT team, should be able to access passwords, etc. in plaintext.

Encryption can also be used to validate someone's identity, such as when sending an email. Digital signatures, another form of cryptography, verify the authenticity and protect the content of the email, which assures the recipient that the contents have not been tampered with and that the sender is authentic. They can also be a suitable solution for any other kind of electronically transmitted information, such as electronic payments. Using a digital signature assures both sender and recipient that the contents have not been tampered with since origination, and also verifies the identity of the sender for the recipient's benefit.

Whatever solution you are leaning towards, it is important to have a clear idea of what you intend to use it for: do you want to protect machines, communications or the Cloud, for example, and are you trying to protect information at rest, in transit or both? Each purpose will likely require a different solution. For securing communications, you probably want to look at HTTPS and/or email encryption. For securing laptops, you should consider hard drive encryption.

12.7.2 Pseudonymisation and anonymisation

For PII – data could directly or indirectly identify specific individuals – anonymisation and pseudonymisation could be good alternatives to encryption, particularly for processing activities that are often 'active', requiring the information to be available in plaintext (rather than in encrypted form). They are similar methodologies but have one key difference: pseudonymised data can be re-identified, whereas anonymised data cannot.

Pseudonymisation means that you process the data in a way that does not identify specific individuals, but those individuals can be re-identified by combining that data with other information that is stored separately and securely. As such, encryption may still be involved for storing that separate information securely while the rest of the information can be processed as the organisation requires.

Anonymisation means that you remove the identifying data or change it in such a way that it cannot identify the individuals to whom it relates. In practice, however, complete anonymisation is often not possible, so if your process makes it at least impossible for your target audience – and unlikely for anyone else – to re-identify the individuals in question, it is normally considered a form of anonymisation. Depending on where you are based, it may also be a criminal act to re-identify, or attempt to re-identify, anonymised data.

You can use a range of techniques for anonymising data, including:

- Deleting or otherwise destroying data that might identify the subject;
- Approximating the data in such a way that the data subject can no longer be identified (for example, reducing dates of birth to only state the year or addresses to only state the county, which still makes the data suitable for research purposes)[66]; and
- Only displaying certain data as totals rather than as individual items.

To pseudonymise data, you typically replace data categories that could identify an individual (e.g. name, address, identification numbers, date of birth) with a 'key' – usually a unique, coded reference – and keep the original information in a different system or location, often secured

[66] Note that the full, original information must not be stored anywhere; otherwise, this would be considered pseudonymisation.

with encryption. Like with the encryption keys discussed earlier in 12.7.1, keeping that key safe is essential to make sure that the pseudonymised data cannot be used by unauthorised individuals to re-identify the data subjects.

The distinction between pseudonymisation and anonymisation, whether it is still (meant to be) possible for specific individuals to be re-identified or not, is important for legal reasons: since personal data specifically refers to data that identifies or can be used to identify specific individuals, data that has been properly anonymised does not qualify as personal data, making it exempt from data protection laws such as the EU GDPR. However, it is important to be sure that it is virtually impossible to re-identify the subjects.

The decision as to what technique to use should be made early on in the process lifecycle. Not only will this minimise the risk in the earlier stages (for example, if the data has not yet been anonymised or pseudonymised), but it will also help enforce the 'privacy by design and default' and 'secure by design' principles discussed in 12.8.

Anonymisation is generally a good option where the data is used for research purposes, whether scientifically or in a market research context. Pseudonymisation can also be a good option for research, but in a situation where you want to protect individuals' identity to a certain audience – for example, presenting research results externally or in a meeting – while still wanting to maintain the ability to re-identify them when required. This is common in a healthcare context, where you might want to make current data available for research purposes but still need to make it possible for a GP or specialist to be able to access their patient's medical history.

12.7.3 Key management

As mentioned several times in this chapter, for any encryption to be effective and to keep the encrypted information secure, it is vital to keep the decryption key safe. Clearly, if an unauthorised individual manages to access that key (as well as the information it can decrypt), the confidentiality and potentially integrity of that information has been breached.

However, protecting the key is also essential for the sake of availability: if any authorised individuals are unable to access the key for whatever reason, perhaps because the key was prematurely destroyed, they will be unable to access or read the encrypted information, rendering it useless. Even if this is arguably less serious than having the information fall into the wrong hands, it is still considered a breach of security, and could be anything from an inconvenience to a finable offence.

When making decisions about key management, it is important to recognise that it is not just about having the technical implementation knowledge, but it is just as much about knowing what questions to ask. These might include:

- How will keys be generated for different cryptographic systems and different applications?
- How will public key certificates be generated and obtained? (Be sure to use a recognised certification authority.)
- How will keys be distributed to authorised users and how will they be activated?
- How and where will keys be stored, and how can authorised users access them?

- How should key-related activity be logged, monitored and audited?
- How frequently should keys and logs be reviewed, and who will be responsible for these reviews?
- How should keys be archived, as the encrypted information may need to be accessed and decrypted at a later date?
- Since you may have to provide access to a key and/or the encrypted material in the event of a court order, how should such legal requests be handled?
- How should keys be revoked, withdrawn or deactivated, and when? (For example, when a key user leaves the organisation.)
- How and when should keys be destroyed, if at all, and on what authorisation?
- How will (suspected) compromised keys be handled?
- How should lost or corrupted keys be recovered so that the encrypted information can be retrieved?

Answers to these questions should be recorded in the encryption policy discussed in 12.7.1.

12.8 System security

> Systems should be designed with security in mind from the earliest stages. Deploying third-party systems should also take security by design into account.
>
> **Key output:** Security by design processes, including regular reviews.

There is often a disconnect between a system's security and users' continuous demands for more flexibility and functionality. Those demands often require systems to be complex. Unfortunately, the more complex a system, the more difficult it is to make it secure. Especially with the time pressure that developers tend to be under, designing something necessarily complex to meet those demands inevitably leads to mistakes, oversights and, ultimately, vulnerabilities. Moreover, a complex system tends to be less user-friendly, and where something – such as security settings – is difficult to use or understand, users are more likely to avoid it.

The fact that security is often treated as an afterthought when developing new technologies does not help that disconnect – only 36% of organisations involve cyber security at the planning stage of a new business initiative.[67] Moreover, belatedly trying to make something secure is typically not just ineffective, but is also more expensive. (The afterthought treatment is also true for inventions in general – it took several decades for car locks to become the norm, for instance.)

12.8.1 Security by design

The prominence of very basic security flaws led to the concepts of 'secure by design' and 'privacy by design and by default' becoming more widespread in recent years. They are also encouraged by governments, including those of the EU and the UK; the UK government's initiative was driven by the growing number of IoT devices, which bring "huge

---

[67] Ernst & Young (EY), "EY Global Information Security Survey2020", February 2020, *https://assets.ey.com/content/dam/ey-sites/ey-com/en_gl/topics/advisory/ey-global-information-security-survey-2020.pdf*.

opportunities" but many consumer devices "lack even basic security provisions".[68] The idea of security by design is that products and services are designed with security in mind from the earliest stages, whether it is something completely new or an innovative use of existing technology.

As an example, a state-of-the-art plug-and-play video conference room solution that includes interactive whiteboarding was found to have multiple major vulnerabilities. Given that it is extremely likely that this technology is used to discuss and display highly confidential information, it is reasonable for consumers to expect an adequate level of security to be built in. Unfortunately, a third party discovered that data was exposed via a publicly accessible Cloud service that lacked encryption, among other flaws, some of which were still not fixed five months after discovery.[69]

As security pioneer Bruce Schneier put it[70]:

> These aren't subtle vulnerabilities. These are stupid design decisions made by engineers who had no idea how to create a secure system. And this, in a nutshell, is the problem with the Internet of Things.

---

[68] Department for Digital, Culture, Media & Sport, "Secure by Design report: Improving the cyber security of consumer Internet of Things Report", March 2018, *https://www.gov.uk/government/publications/secure-by-design-report*.

[69] Forescout Research Labs, "Forescout Research Labs Discovers Multiple Vulnerabilities in DTEN Conferencing and Collaboration Systems", December 2019, *https://www.forescout.com/company/blog/dten-vulnerability/*.

[70] Schneier on Security, "Lousy IoT Security", December 2019, *https://www.schneier.com/blog/archives/2019/12/lousy_iot_secur.html*.

Unfortunately, the problem is not limited to the IoT. Engineers are constantly coming up with innovative systems, whether in the form of a new mobile or web application, hardware, IoT or something else entirely, that are designed to make life easier. Of course, that is only the case if the system functions as it should – and with the cyber landscape as it is, achieving that means designing and executing the innovation with security in mind. For that, threat analysis is key. Conduct risk assessments (see 12.12), consider the threat landscape and your attack surface, and look at incoming intelligence (see 13.1). Consider how the proposed system might fail or be attacked, and how you can mitigate those failures and prevent those attacks without impacting functionality. Then, you can build the necessary security controls and measures into the system.

For example, if you wanted to develop a mobile application that could turn on the heating at home remotely – in other words, create Internet-controlled thermostats – you would need to put a network interface on the home thermostat and design a Cloud service that allows users (via their phones) to communicate with that thermostat. A secure-by-design approach would require you to think about points such as:

- Can the network interface support encryption?
    - Since supporting encryption takes processing power, is a more powerful processor needed?
    - An encryption solution adequate now might not be adequate later (as new vulnerabilities are constantly being discovered), so how can we update the firmware?
- How will authentication work?

- If the switch has no means of putting in a password, authentication needs to happen differently, perhaps by allowing only approved end-user devices to communicate with the thermostat. This requires things such as digital IDs and certificates.
- Since digital IDs and certificates need to be supported by a secure public key infrastructure (PKI), does the storage space need to be increased in order to make room?
- Since a PKI requires updating, does the firmware need to be changed to accommodate for this?

Overcoming encryption and authentication challenges are not your only concerns – there is also the matter of accidental, non-malicious availability issues. What does the system or device do if the communication is cut? Does it store the data locally and upload it when the connection returns? Can it internally assume or predict behaviour based on past actions? Connectivity issues for one reason or another are inevitable, and your system still needs to function to a reasonable standard in those circumstances.

To give a real-life example, when the Cloud service supporting an Internet-connected pet feeder went down, a number of pets went hungry for up to a week.[71] Had the manufacturers thought ahead and considered security by design, the pet feeders could have downloaded and locally stored a feeding schedule and at certain intervals, when connected to the Internet, checked that it reflected the latest

---

[71] BBC News, "Pets 'go hungry' after smart feeder goes offline", February 2020, *https://www.bbc.co.uk/news/technology-51628795*.

data. Where an Internet schedule is not available, the pet feeder can just keep working to the previous, local schedule. Considering that mechanical pet feeders pre-date the Internet-connected ones (and were still produced at the time of the server incident), this type of internal functionality is certainly possible, and likely what customers expect.

12.8.2 Reviewing existing systems

Where you already have systems that were not designed with security in mind, or that were but are due a review, many of the 'security by design' principles still apply. For instance, (re-)analyse the risks: what threats might target your systems? How might your systems fail? It is also worth conducting vulnerability scans (see 13.1.2) and penetration tests (see 13.1.3), and mitigating any weaknesses identified (these are often related to configuration and patch management, also see 12.6).

There are some general threats to look out for depending on the type of system you are trying to secure. For instance, for a web service or another data-driven application, you need to sanitise user inputs properly to prevent SQL injection attacks and stop unauthorised users from gaining access to confidential data. As another example, for the IoT, you need to be wary of communications being intercepted (see 12.9 for network and communications security), for which encryption may be an appropriate solution (see 12.7).

12.8.3 Third-party considerations

Where you rely on a third-party system, make sure that the SLAs provide reassurances of security by design. This might be in the form of records of risk assessments and a broad outline of the measures implemented. You should also check your SLAs for a number of other points, which are discussed in more detail in 12.13.2.

Your procurement processes likely already require you to set out what you need your software and systems to achieve. These can be extended to also set out your security requirements – what encryption is necessary? Does it need to be compatible with your SSO solution? Does it need to support MFA? What customisable controls do you need? Asking these sorts of questions will help you determine whether the system or software meets your security needs.

12.9 Network and communications security

The corporate network should be designed with security in mind, using appropriate technologies and processes such as segmentation and segregation.

Key output: Defined security zones that meet the organisation's security requirements, with appropriate technical measures (such as firewalls and DMZs) in place to form internal perimeters, as well as the external perimeter, covering the entire corporate network.

Before you can look into securing your networks and communications – or, for that matter, anything else – you need to know exactly what you are securing and where it is stored, and follow the secure-by-design principles discussed in 12.8.1. What devices are on your networks? What information do you store and/or process on those devices? Is that information considered to be personal data, or valuable in another way? What are the implications of confidentiality, integrity and/or availability issues? Answering such questions, usually as part of your risk assessment (see 12.12), will help you organise your assets into different security zones based on their security requirements – we discuss this process in more detail in 12.9.1.

However, remember that the 'cyber' side of things is only one aspect of information security – the human aspect is important too, meaning that you should put confidentiality agreements or non-disclosure agreements (NDAs) in place where appropriate. A determined attacker might also take a more physical approach by attempting to connect directly to your networks, so you may need to look into ways of securing wireless routers, network ports (particularly those in semi-public areas, such as meeting rooms and reception areas) and network cabling (often kept in insecure cabinets).

Note that, as network and communications security is a relatively technical CRF process, specialist knowledge and expertise to set up and maintain your networks is particularly essential (also see 12.10). You will need someone skilled in architecture to design your network, as well as someone who is good with segmentation, firewalls, routing, etc. to do the physical work. You should also produce network diagrams for the benefit of both technical staff and staff who are responsible for regulatory compliance. Such diagrams should clearly explain the security zones and show that they are being individually protected.

12.9.1 Creating security zones

As discussed in the introduction, you need to consider what assets you keep on your networks, and group them by security requirement to create security zones. Servers that need to be available 100% of the time, for instance, could be grouped together in one zone, while servers that you can afford to be unavailable for a few hours should be grouped in another, as the measures required for each will be different. In a similar logic, PII, like client and HR data, should be in a different zone from ordinary confidential business information, and a distinction should be drawn between sensitive and non-sensitive personal data, as they have different security requirements.

If you keep all your assets in just one zone (this is known as a 'flat network'), you risk your whole network collapsing if a single vulnerability is exploited. Moreover, it will be harder to pinpoint – and therefore more difficult and expensive to investigate and resolve – any IT incidents (whether caused by a cyber attack or not). Finally, applying the same security measures to all assets will prove either inadequate to meet all security requirements, or more expensive than necessary.

On the flip side, creating a lot of zones requires resources and can make your networks very complex to manage (although virtual local area networks (VLANs) can help reduce equipment complexity by using logical rather than physical networks for segmentation). However, your priorities should lie with creating the number of zones that your security requirements demand. In the longer term, the financial cost of a few extra man hours[72] to set your networks up will almost certainly be balanced out, if not outweighed, by the money you save by resolving incidents quickly (if you

[72] Your network switch, a hardware device with multiple ports that receives incoming data and directs it to the intended destinations, should be able to support hundreds of zones, so there should not be any additional equipment costs.

know in exactly what segment the anomaly was detected, you have fewer machines to check individually), the fact that those incidents are smaller to begin with and mitigating the risks of bad press and fines.

12.9.2 Segmentation and segregation

After you have decided how to divide your assets into different zones and what the requirements for each are, you can look into designing your network to support those requirements, including the security measures necessary for each zone.

An important step in network design is to create network 'segments', each of which has its own private IP address range. This has advantages such as improved performance (reduced traffic on each segment), better containment of network problems (local failures should have limited effect on other segments) and, of course, improved security by routing traffic to only where it needs to go.

After you have segmented your network, you should assign each segment or groups of segments to your security zones, and write rules about what traffic is permitted to flow from and into each zone in order to meet the security requirements you have already established. This stage of network design, referred to as 'segregation', will help enforce your access controls (see 12.4) and reduce the impact of a breach, since you are effectively creating additional internal perimeters. This will make it easier to give users access to only the information they require as well as slow down an attacker trying to move through your networks, buying you more time to detect their activities and stop them before too much damage is done.

Segregation can be realised in several ways, such as by using firewalls (see 12.9.3), DMZs (see 12.9.4) and access control lists. Where possible, you should follow the principles of zero-trust architecture (see 12.9.5).

12.9.3 Firewalls

Earlier, in 12.5.5, firewalls were discussed in the context of anti-malware protection: by setting the default firewall rule to 'deny' and enforcing a whitelist with authorised protocols, ports and applications, your firewall will work as a filter that protects your boundaries, analysing all traffic before it is permitted onto your networks, and stopping any traffic that might be malicious. In effect, a firewall is the gatekeeper: the barrier between your internal networks, which need to remain secure, and the Internet, which should be treated with caution. Firewalls can also be used for internal perimeters, between security zones, to control the flow of traffic and ensure only authorised users and devices can access confidential data.

12.9.4 DMZs

Where a firewall works as a barrier or filter between your networks and the Internet, a DMZ works like a buffer zone between public and private access. A DMZ is a small, isolated network segment located at your organisation's external perimeter (gateway), in which you should place your public-facing servers such as web and email. If you use both a DMZ and a firewall, the result should look something like Figure 1.

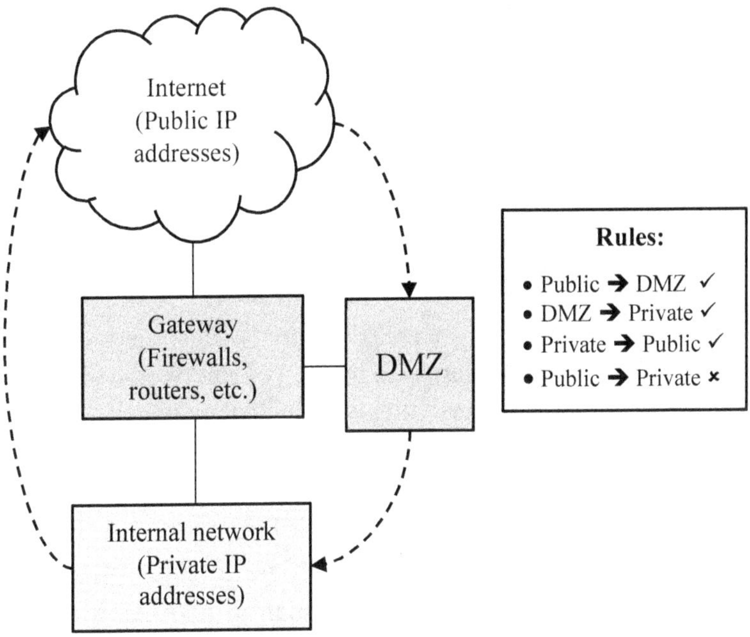

Figure 1: Basic diagram of an organisation's perimeter, with associated traffic rules

You should have rules in place that ensure all external traffic passes through your DMZ for assessment before it can enter your internal networks. Those rules should also ensure that anyone outside your networks, including external threats, can see your public IP addresses only, keeping your private IP addresses hidden.

12.9.5 Zero-trust architecture

It is important to be aware that firewalls and DMZs can only protect you from external threats originating from the Internet. They cannot protect you from the threats that are already inside your networks, having bypassed your firewalls and the rest of your perimeter. Moreover, the internal threat, which was discussed in more detail in chapter 8, is not limited to careless or malicious employees – it could also be an attacker who has hacked a legitimate user's account, for instance, or the intruder who has managed to bypass your firewalls in a different way to gain direct access to your private network. To help mitigate these risks, where possible, follow the principles of 'zero-trust' architecture.

Historically, networks were commonly designed on the assumption that if someone is inside your network, they are 'trusted' to access everything within that network – yet a common theme in security breaches is that of an attacker, once they have gained a foothold in your networks, starting to elevate their privileges to ultimately access highly sensitive data and/or business-critical systems.

In a zero-trust environment, information and services are protected by strong identification, authentication and authorisation solutions (see 12.4) at the external perimeter when first logging in *and* at the internal perimeters between security zones when accessing that information. In other words, access control moves from a single occurrence (entering the overall network) to multiple instances (entering individual security zones) within your internal network, with specific measures appropriate to the data held. Under a zero-trust architecture, permissions to access resources outside your immediate environment, such as in the Cloud or on a network server, are denied by default – you must request access, which is then only granted provided there is justification for you to access it, and this access is only granted for a limited time.

12.10 Security competence and training

> Staff with a security role or security responsibilities have the right competences and qualifications to carry out their duties. These security activities can also be outsourced.
>
> **Key output:** Processes for identifying, developing and maintaining necessary competence.

Besides the everyday security-related duties, such as using a secure password or making sure you close the door behind you, there are dedicated security roles that have responsibilities for implementing security measures, technological or otherwise, and/or performing activities that are purely security-focused, such as reviewing access logs or assessing vulnerability patches. Owners of processes that have direct security implications, such as data processing activities, can also be described as having a security role or security responsibilities.

For small businesses, many of these security activities are likely to be provided by an external resource (also see 12.10.3), while for larger organisations it will often fall to IT and perhaps a senior manager who has the authority to direct in the event of an incident (also see 14.1.1). Internal responsibilities should be spread across both senior management and operational levels, and could be ongoing duties, performed at regular intervals, or only as and when required. Whether you keep the activity internal or outsource it, you need to know how to identify your competence needs.

12.10.1 Roles and responsibilities to consider

The responsibilities you have to define and assign will depend on your legal and contractual obligations, as well as your business requirements, which in turn inform what other security measures you need to put in place. For example, if you have determined that you need to encrypt your PII databases, you will need someone who can advise on the benefits and drawbacks of different encryption solutions and help you implement them.

Whatever your specific requirements, however, many organisations will require some form of IT helpdesk. These are usually the people who will deal with implementing and maintaining most technological measures, and will also generally be the first point of contact when an incident occurs, who can then escalate as appropriate.

Under some jurisdictions, there will also be legal requirements for specific roles with specific competences, such as an EU GDPR data protection officer (DPO).[73] Regardless of whether you need a DPO, most modern data protection legislation will require you to assign responsibilities for communicating with data subjects and relevant authorities, conducting data protection or privacy impact assessments, etc. Most of these responsibilities require specialised skills and ideally practical experience.

For implementing cyber security, you should also consider the competence required of the project manager in charge of the implementation project, and the senior manager responsible for maintaining the later security programme. This also means being aware of the organisation's

[73] EU GDPR, Section 4, Articles 37–39.

requirements as they change over time and how to address them. These managers do not necessarily need the technical knowledge to understand, for example, the different types of encryption and the benefits of each, but should be aware of the more general principles (such as what encryption is supposed to achieve, and in what circumstances it should be considered). They should also know what questions to ask to ensure those principles and relevant objectives are met.

12.10.2 Developing competence

Having identified the roles and responsibilities that are required, you also need to establish the specific skills and competences those roles require. A good starting point is asking the person you intend to assign about the resources, in the form of tools or training, they require. Looking up relevant job descriptions can also point you in the right direction if you have no one to ask.

Where competence needs to be developed, consider options such as:

- Formal training in the form of certification or a degree;
- Simple training activities;
- Technological assistance; and
- Outsourcing (see 12.10.3).

Simply gaining experience may also be vital to developing the right competence, but is often paired with training, whether formal or not. Where the training is formal, however, certifications provide easy evidence of competence. Such qualifications might also be contractually or legally mandated.

Where you have specialised staff, it is also important to maintain their competence. Offering regular training will help keep their skills and knowledge up to date. It will also demonstrate your interest in their career, encouraging them to stay with your organisation.

12.10.3 Outsourcing considerations

Outsourcing certainly brings benefits, particularly for smaller organisations. It can prove cheaper than having in-house expertise, especially if your cyber security requirements do not demand a full-time position.

Furthermore, deciding to rely on an external supplier often means being able to access some of the best expertise – a dedicated team of experts who stay on top of the latest industry news, and can offer their service as well as select appropriate products and tools to help them deliver that service. Depending on your level of engagement, this can also help you develop the necessary competence within your organisation.

12.11 Staff awareness training

> Employees receive regular cyber security awareness training, and know how to recognise and respond to security threats. Security should also be embedded in the organisation's culture.
>
> **Key output:** Established staff awareness training programme with clearly defined and measurable learning objectives.

For several processes in this chapter, we mentioned staff awareness training, and how it can significantly improve your organisation's security posture. Note that this is the general awareness training that all staff and contractors should receive, and not the specialised training talked about in 12.10.

Here, we will talk about training more generally, what training options exist, how to measure training in an auditable way and how to build a security culture throughout your organisation.

12.11.1 Developing staff awareness

A starting point for developing security awareness is establishing a reliable programme for delivering training. For most organisations, this means rolling out security awareness training to all staff at their induction, followed by at least annual refreshers. In particular, it is critical to teach them that even in a non-technical or non-security-specific role, they – and every other individual in the company – are responsible for security. The training should also teach them how they can contribute to good security.

Remember, however, that awareness training is just that – it is not a guarantee that your staff will always act correctly or in a timely fashion, but it does ensure that each of them knows what should be done, and that is the foundation of good security behaviour.

12.11.2 Determining your training needs

Determining your – and your learners' – training needs starts with asking yourself why you are looking for staff awareness training in the first place. What are you trying to make staff aware of? What type of incident(s) are you trying to prevent? Are you concerned about suspicious events not being reported internally? 'Security training' can cover a broad range of topics, including teaching staff:

- How to choose a strong password and keep it secure;
- How to recognise a phishing email;
- To lock their screens when they are not at their desks;
- About the risks of public Wi-Fi;
- To shred (or otherwise destroy) any confidential papers left in printers;
- To challenge any strangers on the premises; and
- To report any known or suspected security breaches.

This is far from an exhaustive list, but should give you an idea of the wide range of learning objectives you could consider, depending on the problems you are trying to solve or incidents you want to prevent. Looking at your organisation's incident history (regardless of whether they caused any actual harm) could help you determine what you might need to cover in your staff training.

A good training provider will provide information on the topics covered or a syllabus before you have to commit to a purchase.

12.11.3 Training options

The problems you are trying to solve, which should determine the specifics of the topics to address and how in-depth the training should be, are not your only consideration. Learner requirements (or preferences) and budget are equally important – and the matter of budget can be further complicated by having to think about how many people you intend to train and how often the training should be repeated (which will depend on your organisation's risk appetite, see 12.12.6).

There are three broad security awareness training options currently popular and widely available – classroom training, live online training and e-learning – and each comes with its own benefits, which are broadly summarised in Table 3. Some delivery methods are more cost-effective, others give learners the opportunity to ask questions, etc. – the 'best' option will depend on your requirements and priorities. Ultimately, the best delivery method for you will depend on your requirements – how much information you want employees to have, how many employees require the training, any additional topics you need to address besides general cyber and information security (such as the EU GDPR), your budget, etc.

Table 3: Benefits of Different Training Options

	Classroom	**Live online**	**E-learning**
Trainer-led	✓	✓	
Easy to engage	✓		✓
Can ask questions/get clarification	✓	✓	
Cost-effective		✓	✓
Can take wherever convenient		✓	✓
Can take whenever convenient			✓

In a trainer-led course, the trainer has direct contact with the attendees (especially in a classroom setting) – this should make it easier for them to gauge learners' reactions, such as confusion, and appropriately respond to them by re-explaining a concept or taking a different approach. However, this strongly depends on the trainer's skill and mental state on the day of the training. Additionally, where employees are split into different training groups, each may not receive the exact same explanations (and possibly a different trainer altogether), which could mean that the training given is not consistent across the organisation despite the same learning materials.

As for engagement, just watching one, long presentation is more likely to be boring (and not give learners the chance to truly absorb the information) than breaking it up with regular exercises. E-learning courses can be made engaging with similar exercises, in addition to letting the learner click through the course at their own pace. On the other hand, in a live online environment, attendees and the trainer inevitably cannot see each other face to face – possibly not see each other at all, just the presentation – so full engagement can require a lot more effort. Additionally, getting people out of the office generally makes for a better learning environment, since this helps them disengage from their day-to-day work, helping them fully concentrate on their learning.

The biggest benefits of the digital training options – live online and e-learning – are convenience and cost-effectiveness. You will not need to halt productivity for a whole or half a day while your employees disappear for their training, incur travel or accommodation costs, or pay more to get a trainer on site. Additional benefits of e-learning are that you do not need to pay for the trainer's time at all, and that employees can choose the time they study or complete the training in several sessions.

Remember that training should not be a one-off investment – people can be forgetful, particularly about matters that do not come up every day, so refresher training at least annually is a good idea. That said, even with regular refreshers and good intentions, training is easy to forget at the end of a busy working day. It may therefore be worth supplementing standard staff training with well-placed visual reminders (such as posters) and sending all-staff emails, warning, for example, that a particular phishing email or call is targeting the organisation.

12.11.4 Measuring training

Another critical aspect of effective training is measurement – and not in an anecdotal way, or by randomly asking a handful of employees whether they have completed the training and what they thought of it, but in a way that is useful to the organisation. Records of measurement can also be useful for presenting to an auditor or a regulator. Even if you are not expecting any such checks, you may be subject to an investigation after a breach, in which case you need to be able to demonstrate that you have taken reasonable action to prevent the incident.

When measuring the effectiveness of training via, for example, a test at the end of the course, it is important to refer back to the earlier learning objectives and the incidents you are trying to prevent. For instance, if you wanted to prevent staff from falling for phishing attacks, the corresponding learning objective might be to ensure they can recognise a suspicious email. The test or exercise that measures learner understanding might ask the learner to identify whether example emails are phishing or legitimate. If the objective is also to ensure learners know how to report the email, the test's questions might ask about follow-up actions, having identified the email as phishing.

It is also important to be aware of the limitations of tests. For instance, there is a risk that as soon as staff have passed their test, they stop thinking about – or outright forget[74] – what they have learned. For instance, simulated phishing campaigns (see 13.1.2) can help confirm that staff are able to recognise and appropriately respond to a phishing email. Building a security culture (see 12.11.5) and clear board-level commitment to security (see 15.4) will also help improve staff awareness and ensure they take security seriously.

12.11.5 Building a security culture

For staff across the organisation to truly take note of security and apply the knowledge gained from any training, security should be embedded in your company's culture. In other words, you should aim to build a 'security culture'. However, before you can think about how to build and influence any organisation's security culture, it is important to first understand what a security culture is.

Since security is about being free from danger or threat, and a culture is the collected ideas, behaviours and customs of a group of people, a 'security culture' could be defined as the ideas, behaviours and customs of a group of people that protects them from danger or threat.

---

[74] Ebbinghaus's forgetting curve shows that it is natural for information that we have just learned to disappear at an exponential rate.

This can work both positively and negatively: in an organisation where most employees leave their unattended computer unlocked, the few who are not yet in that habit may quickly follow suit, as will any newcomers to that organisation. Similarly, if it is common practice for a door to be wedged open most days, that may quickly extend to *all* days. Worse, it might be left open overnight, too. However, adopting a positive culture could happen if, for example, existing employees clearly challenge any unfamiliar faces, new joiners will likely observe this and feel more comfortable doing the same.

The strength of the culture is also a factor that affects employee behaviour: where it is strong, newcomers are more likely to adopt it, and adopt it quickly. However, a weak culture might never truly be adopted by everyone or, in more extreme cases, be changed by newcomers' ways.

The strength of a security culture – and the specifics of that culture – are not just down to the people; the other two security pillars – processes and technology – also contribute to it. An organised society relies on authority, and individuals tend to appreciate this (some studies even suggest that our brains are hardwired for it[75]). This means they generally tend to abide by laws and rules – including those in the form of policies or procedures – provided they

[75] According to this study, ten-month old infants – who are too young to communicate verbally – recognise when two novel agents have conflicting goals and use those agents' relative size to predict the outcome of the collision. Full study available at: Lotte Thomsen et al., "Big and Mighty: Preverbal Infants Mentally Represent Social Dominance", *Science* 331 (6016), January 2011, *https://www.ncbi.nlm.nih.gov/pmc/articles/PMC3860821*.

seem sensible and fair. Enforcement is easier still if your technology helps them follow those rules.

Also remember that the culture and general atmosphere must remain healthy, so avoid punishment for things such as reporting breaches; otherwise, you may create a culture of fear in which breaches go unreported and unaddressed for longer, which exponentially increases the damage to your organisation. To avoid such situations, create a culture based on openness – actively encouraging employees to speak up and praising them (or otherwise recognising that they have done the right thing) when they do are both important steps in building that healthy security culture.

The stronger and healthier your security culture, the stronger – and often more mature – your organisation's security will be as a whole. Embedding security in your organisation's culture will also help people see why security training is necessary, and being praised for applying what they learned will work motivationally and help embed the knowledge gained.

Since the cost of building this kind of culture is often financially small compared to the potential benefit, it is almost certainly a worthwhile investment. However, remember that building and maintaining a security culture (or, for that matter, any other kind of culture) requires a team and top-down effort.

12.12 Comprehensive risk management programme

Identifying, assessing and responding to cyber and information security risks in a structured and methodical manner, as part of a wider risk management programme.

Key output: Comprehensive and structured risk assessments conducted on a regular basis.

For most CRF processes, conducting a risk assessment is a critical part of identifying the specific measures to implement. Performing a risk assessment is also a necessary step for effectively implementing the overall Framework, since it will help you make sensible and cost-effective decisions on what processes to consider in the first place, which is why it is a separate step in our eight-step approach to implementing cyber security (see step 6, chapter 23).

Even though risk assessments are conducted in many organisations, relatively few conduct them in a truly structured, methodical manner that ensures the results are justifiable, consistent across different areas of the business and repeatable.

Of course, any kind of risk assessment is a first step to efficient defences, and even an unstructured or intuitive approach is probably better than nothing at all. Whatever the approach, risk assessment is an effective way of working out exactly what threats and vulnerabilities can harm your organisation the most, and helping you decide which ones to address first.

However, conducting that risk assessment in a comprehensive, structured and more formal manner brings additional advantages. It helps ensure the process can be applied consistently by different people, which will help you appropriately prioritise risk treatments. A structured approach also makes it less likely you will overlook any risks.

A formal programme also makes it easier to plan risk assessment reviews, at regular intervals and when planning (or already having made) big changes, and make sure these are conducted as planned. Your programme might also consist of multiple risk assessments, perhaps divided up on a departmental basis, which can be grouped by review intervals, methodology, etc.

The actual approach or methodology your organisation chooses does not particularly matter, as long as it can ensure valid, repeatable and comparable results, and is an approach that suits your business needs. There are some principles your methodology should observe to ensure effective risk analysis and treatment, however, which are discussed in 12.12.1.

12.12.1 Risk assessment methodology

Put simply, a risk is a vulnerability exploited by a threat, which is why the following formula, or some variation of it, is often used in risk assessment:

threat x vulnerability = risk

A different way of stating it is:

event x trigger = consequence

No matter the wording, the key is that you answer the questions 'how?' (a threat or event), 'why?' (a vulnerability or trigger) and 'so what?' (the risk or consequence). For example, if an attacker exploits a vulnerability (threat/how) in software that you have not updated (vulnerability/why), data might end up stolen (risk/so what).

However, just as risk assessment can be used to protect the organisation, it can also be used to assess the relative benefits of a risky activity. For instance, launching a new service that involves more data collection may make you a more attractive target to cyber criminals, which increases the risk of a more serious data breach, but that risk might be balanced against the increased profit generated by the new service, which in turn could allow for greater investment in security controls to mitigate the increased risk. As another example, allowing employees to use their personal devices for work purposes may introduce a security risk, but could nonetheless be the sensible thing to do if you have a tight budget (although you should mitigate the risk at least partially by introducing a BYOD policy).

This is a fairly straightforward approach, but it provides the basis to gather information to analyse and understand the risk and, if necessary, address it in an informed manner. With the earlier out-of-date software example, the basic answer would probably be to update that software. Better still would be to look at the bigger picture and address the root cause of the problem by automating updates for all software and, even better, review all your software to check if you still need them all and whether they are supported, then retiring or replacing unsupported or unneeded software.

Such an analysis and treatment would not be possible if, as is a relatively easy trap to fall into, risks were written down in general statements such as 'data breach', 'loss of business', 'brand damage' or 'GDPR fine'. The problem with this approach is that it looks at the consequences rather than the circumstances that lead to those consequences. To use the latter example, you should not be asking yourself what the risk of being fined under the GDPR is, but what actions or events could lead to those fines.

12.12.2 Identifying risks

It can be difficult to know how to identify the threats and vulnerabilities that comprise risks, as well as ensure you are looking at the right risks. Naturally, you do not want to overlook any risks, especially the higher-level ones that require treatment, but you also need to make sure that you do not spend too much time addressing risks that will not significantly impact what you are doing, whether they materialise or not – this seems very obvious, but is nonetheless an easy mistake to make when trying to be comprehensive (also see 12.12.3). Key to avoiding this is having a clearly defined scope that accounts for the assets you are trying to protect, your business context (such as your sector), and the stakeholder, regulatory, contractual and operational requirements that you must meet. It is also important to prioritise the right risks, for which you should look at your threat landscape and intelligence (see 13.1).

To help focus the risk assessment and avoid straying too far into unrelated territory, conduct multiple smaller assessments. By limiting the scope for each assessment, conducting a separate one for network-related risks, Cloud-related risks, etc., you will find it easier to clearly define and stick to each scope. However you split them up, combining your smaller scopes should account for all your assets and requirements.

By defining the scope of a given assessment in a relatively narrow way, you can also keep the number of requirements you need to account for at a manageable level. Cloud service risks, for example, will likely centre around data security, privacy and PII protection, hardware reliability and uptime requirements, alongside more prosaic items such as server-room cooling or backup power supplies. Taking a more focused approach like this will ultimately make for better risk assessments.

Once you have defined the scope and relevant requirements, there are generally two approaches you can take to identify relevant risks:

1. ***Asset-based:***

   This approach requires an asset register (see 12.1.2 and appendix 1), a list of business processes (if not included in your asset register) and ideally a database or list of threats and vulnerabilities to consider.

   The idea is that you establish the vulnerabilities of each of your assets and consider the threats that might exploit each of those vulnerabilities. For instance, paperwork (asset) will every now and then need to be taken out of secure storage for active use (vulnerability), where it might be viewed or taken by an unauthorised individual (threat).

   Each 'incident scenario' – the combination of a specific threat exploiting a specific vulnerability – is a clearly defined risk that can be analysed and, if necessary, addressed in the next stage. Asset owners and relevant stakeholders can offer valuable input in this process – they have the best understanding of the asset and how it is used, which naturally impacts susceptibility to the threats identified.

2. ***Scenario-based:***

   In a scenario-based risk assessment, you examine all the consequences of an event – often larger-scale scenarios that are common to many organisations – in a broad fashion. A fire in a key server room, for example, could impact the integrity and availability of a wide range of physical and digital assets and infrastructure, quite apart from health and safety and business continuity concerns, and possible negative media and regulatory attention.

   Defending against fire also requires a broad approach. Are there smoking areas near any flammables, such as shredded paperwork awaiting collection and disposal? Are fire suppression systems installed? Is equipment with significant heat output adequately cooled? Each contributes to your defence, but relying on just one or two measures will probably prove insufficient – it is necessary to account for the whole threat scenario in order to be truly secure.

   Identifying threat scenarios begins with discussions with key persons within the organisation, such as facilities managers, IT managers, etc. They have the clearest overall picture of operations at the scale necessary to conduct scenario-based assessments, as well as valuable experience that can help identify relevant risks and suitable mitigations. Asset owners and lower-level stakeholders may also be able to provide valuable input for the same reasons they can aid an asset-based assessment.

> It is quite possible that not every relevant scenario is identified. This is perfectly acceptable – the point is that you gather enough information to be able to make informed decisions on what measures to implement. That said, where a scenario is raised that, under examination, turns out to be redundant, it should still be recorded for later examination in case the situation changes. The additional information may also help you better understand the risks and prioritise risk responses more effectively.

Neither approach is superior to the other – the 'better' approach depends on your organisation's needs. For example, one limitation of the asset-based approach is that it tends to look at a single threat per risk or incident scenario. If you expect to be targeted by, say, organised crime, it is important to consider combined attack vectors that present more complex threats, for which scenario-based assessments are more suitable.

The scenario-based approach can also work well for smaller organisations or organisations with very specific requirements and obligations (for instance, in the gambling industry, a key concern is preventing fraud, while in publishing, protecting manuscripts or papers from premature release tends to be the priority), as both tend to have a very clear idea of what scenarios they must prevent, and therefore what their critical risks are. On the other hand, if you prefer a more methodical, almost checklist-like approach, conducting an asset-based assessment is probably more suitable.

Arguably the most comprehensive approach is to conduct both asset-based and scenario-based assessments. Starting with an asset-based approach can reduce the workload of the scenario-based assessment conducted later, as some controls necessary to mitigate a given scenario will have already been identified in the asset-based assessment. Starting with the scenario-based assessment, on the other hand, can help you identify asset-based risks you might not have otherwise considered, but may also require you to make changes to your asset-based controls if a particular scenario casts them in a new light.

There is no 'right' method or, if you make use of both methods, no 'right' order – it is simply a matter of choosing what works best for you. Where you choose to make use of both approaches, however, remember that risk assessment should be a cyclic process, where one method informs the other as a matter of course. Moreover, whatever the method, after identifying a risk, do not immediately assume it is the only relevant risk for that asset or scenario. Even if further risks could be mitigated with the same measure, satisfy yourself that you have covered all relevant risks and conducted your due diligence.

12.12.3 Deciding whether the risk is relevant

The wide range of threats that may compromise information security makes for an equally wide range of information security risks. To make sure the risks you have identified really are information security risks, ask yourself whether they could impact the confidentiality, integrity and/or availability of your information assets or systems, as well as their resilience.

It is also important to realise that an information security risk will be viewed differently by different teams within the organisation, as the same risk will impact each team differently depending on their day-to-day responsibilities.

For example, the board will primarily be concerned with strategic impacts, while the IT team will be more concerned with possible impacts on systems and infrastructure.

Looking beyond internal stakeholders, you should also consider the risks that external stakeholders such as suppliers may present (also see 12.13). They do not necessarily have the same investment in security as you, so you may need to assess the relevant risks differently, particularly since in many cases you will be held accountable for a breach at the supplier's end if you have not applied sufficient preventive measures such as requiring them to meet certain standards and conducting due diligence checks.

You should also consider other stakeholders with an interest in your security measures, such as data subjects, since you are responsible for keeping their data safe, and a breach could be more damaging to them than to you (even if recent data privacy legislation is designed to make the consequences of failing to adequately protect personal data more serious). That risk to individuals' rights and freedoms is what data protection watchdogs tend to be most concerned about, so appreciating how data subjects may see or experience the risks of data processing and taking appropriate measures will ultimately also protect your organisation. Conducting data protection or privacy impact assessments can help you determine whether a processing activity might harm a data subject, how likely it is that they might be harmed and the extent of that possible harm.

12.12.4 Risk owners and register

Just as assets should each have an asset owner and be recorded in an asset register, risks should be assigned a risk owner and recorded in a risk register (which should refer to items in the asset register, particularly if you conduct an asset-based risk assessment).

The risk owner will primarily be responsible for making sure any necessary risk treatments (technical controls, policies or procedures, staff training, etc.) are applied and effective, and that any residual risk is acceptable (see 12.12.7). Note that risks are treated in a later stage in the risk assessment process, but the risk owner should be identified before you start assessing the risk levels, since they may be able to provide useful input leading up to that.

Risk owners are also responsible for regularly reviewing the risks and making sure they are still acceptable, and that controls are still working correctly.

Like your asset register, your risk register should list some specifics about each risk, such as:

- Risk owner;
- Original likelihood, impact and overall risk (based on fixed criteria; see below);
- Residual likelihood, impact and overall risk (based on the same criteria);
- Treatment information, or justification for tolerating a risk;
- Target date and responsibilities for completion of actions; and
- When the next review is due.

As you proceed through the next steps of the risk assessment, you will gradually obtain the information to complete the details of your risk register.

12.12.5 Assessing risk levels

Having identified your risks, you need to determine – in a justifiable, structured and consistent way – how significant each risk is. To do that, you need to measure both frequency (how likely is it that the risk will materialise) and impact (how significant are the consequences if the risk does materialise).

Broadly speaking, there are two approaches to risk analysis: quantitative and qualitative. Quantitative assessment attempts to assign a precise numerical value to a risk based on large quantities of data. In many cases there is not enough data to analyse or too many variables are involved, so taking a quantitative approach in information security may be impractical and cost-ineffective. Qualitative assessment, the more common approach in information security, relies on stakeholders' knowledge and experience to determine an 'estimated' risk. This has the drawback of subjectivity, but is much quicker and easier to perform than quantitative assessment, and can often still produce good results. The approach described in this section is a qualitative one.

To establish frequency and impact, you typically define between three and seven risk 'categories', often named something like:

- 'Critical', 'high', 'medium', 'low' and 'negligible';
- 'Almost certain', 'likely', 'possible', 'unlikely' and 'rare'; and
- 'Catastrophic', 'major', 'modest', 'minor' and 'insignificant'.

It does not really matter what category names you choose, as long as you apply them consistently across the organisation. It is also important to give each name a clear description or value, and preferably aligned to multiple types of criteria when measuring impact. Table 4 and Table 5 provide example likelihood and impact criteria.

Table 4: Example Likelihood Criteria

Level	Likelihood	Description
5	Almost certain	Expected weekly.
4	Likely	Expected monthly.
3	Possible	Expected every one or two years.
2	Unlikely	Expected every three to five years.
1	Rare	Expected every five years or less frequent.

Table 5: Example Impact Criteria

Level	Category	Financial impact	Reputational impact
5	Catastrophic	>£5 million	Losing >30% of customers.
4	Major	£2 million – £5 million	Losing 15% – 30% of customers.
3	Modest	£500,000 – £2 million	Losing 5% – 15% of customers.
2	Minor	£100,000 – £500,000	Losing 1% – 5% of customers.
1	Insignificant	<£100,000	Losing <1% of customers.

Clearly, the exact values for each level depend on the size of your organisation and the nature of your business, but it may be a good idea to set an even number of categories so people are forced to choose one of 'medium/bad' or 'medium/good'. Also make sure staff know that where they are not sure about the impact because it can vary depending on how the risk materialises, the worst-case scenario should be assumed – if the risk does materialise, and it turns out that the impact is not as bad as you had prepared for, all the better.

Having established impact and likelihood for each incident scenario, you need to measure the overall risk level. There are different ways of doing this, and generally any method is valid as long as you apply it consistently and it provides useful outputs, but usually the risk 'score' is calculated as some product of impact and likelihood. That risk score can then be visualised in a likelihood–impact (or frequency–impact) matrix such as the one in Table 6.

Table 6: Likelihood–impact Matrix

Likelihood						
	5					
	4					
	3					
	2					
	1					
		1	**2**	**3**	**4**	**5**
		Impact				

The matrix should clearly separate different areas, usually by using colour-coding, to indicate which risks are considered unacceptable (usually 'high' risk), which ones require careful monitoring and more regular reviews ('medium' risk) and which ones are within your risk appetite ('low' risk). Based on these findings, you should prioritise the risks. Any risk that exceeds your risk appetite will require a response (see 12.12.7).

12.12.6 Risk appetite

Your risk appetite is an important point to establish early on in your implementation project (our approach includes it in step 2, see chapter 19). Your risk appetite, or risk tolerance, sets out the level of risk that is acceptable to your organisation. This is based on your requirements and objectives – translating your business, legal and contractual requirements might show, for instance, that you are unwilling to accept any risk above minimum impact, but are able to tolerate a fairly high frequency – which you can adjust based on the resources available if necessary.

Your risk appetite should also reflect how your organisation generally does business. If you generally have a high tolerance for risk, you will likely take the same approach to information and cyber security. Likewise, if you tend to be risk-averse, it makes sense to apply a similar level of caution when it comes to security.

Note that any subsequent likelihood–impact matrix, such as the one above, should reflect that risk appetite, combined with the likelihood and impact criteria you have set. When expressing your risk appetite, you could set a maximum risk score, or set maximum levels individually for impact and likelihood – the most appropriate method will depend on your requirements.

12.12.7 Risk responses

Generally speaking, there are four ways (sometimes referred to as 'the four Ts') you can respond to a risk:

1. **Treat**
   Implementing security controls to reduce the impact and/or likelihood of the risk to an acceptable level. Those controls could be preventive, detective or responsive, or a combination. You do not need to limit yourself to technical controls – staff training, recruiting, and developing (or amending) policies and procedures are all valid ways of reducing a risk. Moreover, applying different types of control can help provide more 'defence in depth' (discussed in more detail in 12.12.8).
2. **Transfer**
   Transferring all or part of the risk to another party, such as through insurance or by outsourcing the process to an organisation that is better able to manage the risk.
3. **Terminate**
   Terminating the source of the threat, perhaps by ending a business activity or changing the way it is done.
4. **Tolerate**
   Actively choosing to tolerate the risk if it is not possible or too expensive to treat the risk, or if it presents an opportunity for a positive outcome.

Make sure that you document your chosen response, including justifications and, where applicable, your chosen controls. Also make sure that the risk owner has agreed to it and is in a position to ensure it will be implemented correctly. After implementation, review the effectiveness of the controls to ensure the risk has been sufficiently mitigated. Remember, you often do not need to (or cannot) eliminate a risk entirely, just lower it to a level that is acceptable to your risk appetite.

Risk owners should also regularly review the risks to make sure they are still acceptable, and review the risk treatments to make sure they are still working and achieving what was intended – particularly if the solution was a technological one, it is possible that it has been rendered invalid by new vulnerabilities or superseded by a more advanced or secure alternative.

Risk assessment and responses are discussed further in steps 6 and 7 of our eight-step approach to implementing cyber security (chapters 23 and 24 respectively).

12.12.8 Defence in depth

No single measure, particularly a preventive one, works 100% of the time, which is why a treated risk is still a risk, just one that is less likely to occur and/or less harmful if it does. Even if your measures are effectively implemented and well-maintained, security can still fail (over the years, and as immortalised in several films, high-security prisons such as Alcatraz Federal Penitentiary have seen escapees, for instance). Therefore, a more dynamic approach, where individual security measures work together effectively and make up for each other's weaknesses, is required.

In a defence-in-depth approach, you have multiple, layered defences in place so that, if one layer fails, the other layers still prevent the attack from succeeding. Ideally, each layer also presents a different challenge for an attacker (think moats and walls for castles).

To go back to the earlier example, many break-out attempts in history were stopped by a second or third layer of security (after breaking through the first layer). In an organisational setting, a receptionist (second layer) might spot an intruder who managed to get through an entrance protected by a PIN code (first layer). As a third layer of defence, if the intruder makes it to the office area, they can be stopped from accessing particularly sensitive data with traditionally locked private offices, drawers and filing cabinets.

The defence in depth concept is not limited to physical security, however. For example, when defending against malware, your primary goal is to stop it from entering your networks at all, so your first layer of defence will consist of measures such as whitelisting and firewalls. Your next layer of defence might aim to prevent malicious code from executing, while a further layer might assume that the code has already been executed and attempt to stop it from spreading further via measures such as segmentation and segregation.

When considering your options in respect of defence in depth, the key is to consider how your controls might be circumvented. That often requires you to find the weakest link in your security, which a smart attacker will find and attempt to exploit. In other words, the strength of your overall security system is equal to the strength of your weakest point. If you want to improve overall security to mitigate the risk, you have to find and strengthen your weakest link.

Be aware, however, that finding your weakest link is no easy task, if only because it will depend on the threat. The weakest link from a physical intruder's perspective, for example, will be very different from a cyber criminal's. Weak links also strongly depend on the attacker's intentions – a common thief is a very different kind of physical intruder from someone who wants to snoop through your data, and different again from someone who wants to infect your systems or install a keylogger.

As a complement to defence in depth, you can make use of 'choke points', whereby you force traffic (whether people or data) into a smaller channel that is easier to secure, as you can focus your resources. If you know where your weak points are, you also know where to look for intruders.

12.13 Supply chain risk management

> Steps are taken, including due diligence checks and appropriate contracts, to ensure the entire supply chain, including physical suppliers, software vendors and Cloud service providers, is secure.
>
> **Key output:** Processes and checklists for checking information-sharing rules and security responsibilities are adequate and clear, and legally enforceable.

Even if your own organisation's security is sound, as discussed in chapter 10 (third-party threats), you can still be vulnerable to attack through any of your suppliers or partners if you do not conduct a certain level of due diligence to ensure that your supply chain is sufficiently secure.

Due diligence is fundamentally a form of risk assessment. Although it is obviously important to assess third parties that can directly access significant amounts of confidential information, such as a partner or Cloud service provider, it is also important not to overlook seemingly cyber-safe services such as a utility provider. Consider the infamous Target attack from 2013 (which is still regularly and widely cited several years after the event), in which 70 million PII records and up to 40 million payment card numbers were stolen by criminal hackers, who initially gained entry to Target's systems with login credentials stolen from its third-party heating, ventilation and air-conditioning provider.[76] The Target incident is discussed in more detail in 10.2.

The third-party weakness was not the sole vulnerability that led to the scale of the data theft – weak segmentation (also see 12.9.2) on Target's end significantly aggravated the breach – emphasising how important it is to not neglect some security aspects in favour of others, and to take a 'defence in depth' approach where possible (see 12.12.8).

12.13.1 Due diligence

Performing due diligence can be the difference between buying an IT asset or buying an IT liability. Mergers and acquisitions can introduce new vulnerabilities, such as when acquiring a system or network that has not been appropriately configured and potentially already breached. This happened to Marriott International when it acquired Starwood Hotels in 2016. Unfortunately, Starwood's systems had been compromised in 2014, but the exposure of

---

[76] Shu Xiaokui et al., "Breaking the Target: An Analysis of Target Data Breach and Lessons Learned", *arXiv:1701.04940*, January 2017, https://arxiv.org/abs/1701.04940.

the customer information on those systems was not discovered until 2018.[77]

Preventing a Target or Marriott scenario starts with knowing what questions to ask when looking to acquire another organisation or seeking a service provider or supplier. Such questions might include:

- How much does the organisation rely on its IT infrastructure, and does the nature of your possible future relationship depend on data transfers and/or service availability?
- What IT audits have been conducted, when did they take place, how reliable are they (did they, for example, lead to a recognised best-practice certification such as ISO 27001) and are you able to see the reports?
- Does the organisation maintain its IT infrastructure properly, and can it prove this, such as with appropriate documentation?
- Can the organisation provide reasonable assurances that appropriate technical and organisational measures are in place to protect its IT infrastructure and any data transfers that might take place between you?
- Does the organisation have a known history of security incidents, and if so, can it demonstrate that those incidents are unlikely to repeat themselves?
- If the organisation cannot provide that assurance, is there a significant risk of a security incident that would

[77] ICO, "Statement: Intention to fine Marriott International, Inc more than £99 million under GDPR for data breach", July 2019, *https://ico.org.uk/about-the-ico/news-and-events/news-and-blogs/2019/07/statement-intention-to-fine-marriott-international-inc-more-than-99-million-under-gdpr-for-data-breach/*.

hinder the organisation's ability to offer its services and/or products? If so, would this hinder your ability to effectively run your business?
- Does the organisation maintain a supplier register?

For possible mergers, you may also need to consider:

- Is any data you would acquire of a good enough quality and in compliance with relevant data protection, privacy and electronic communication laws? Several authorities provide relevant due diligence checklists that could help.[78]
- How easy is it to separate the IT from the parent company? And if separation is not a practical approach, what alternative arrangements will you use?
- Do IT staff have the right skills and knowledge, or will you need to recruit and/or train specialist staff?
- Will the employees fit into your organisation's security culture? And if not, do you need to invest in training and can you afford to give them time to adapt?

12.13.2 Reviewing SLAs

For suppliers and service providers, you should also take the precaution of carefully reviewing your contracts/SLAs, and make sure that they provide guarantees of adequate security and regulatory compliance. Even if the terms and conditions

---

[78] For example, the UK's ICO offers a due diligence checklist for indirect consent when buying a marketing list to help organisations comply with the Privacy and Electronic Communications (EC Directive) Regulations 2003 (PECR). Available at: ICO, "Electronic and telephone marketing", March 2018, *https://ico.org.uk/for-organisations/guide-to-pecr/electronic-and-telephone-marketing/*, paragraph 179.

offer little or no room for negotiation (which is common), you can still check for points such as the following:

- Is the SLA clear about roles and responsibilities for both supplier and customer, including relationships such as between data controller and processor?
- Is the SLA specific about what services are and are not included?
- Does the SLA clearly identify relevant benchmarks and metrics?
- Does the SLA specify what the disputes and problem resolution process is, including escalation processes where necessary?
- What security assurances does the supplier offer? Recognised certification schemes are ideal for these purposes, but be aware of the limitations of self-certified schemes. These do not require verification from an external, independent body, and rely wholly on the organisation's honesty and integrity.

Bear in mind that this is a non-exhaustive, generic list, and more specific checks will depend on the nature of the service being offered. For a Cloud service provider, for instance, you need to make sure that the data you supply is confidential by default.

Finally, remember that due diligence and careful review are important – it is critical to get it right the first time, and failing to do so may prove costly.

CHAPTER 13: IDENTIFY AND DETECT

> Develop a system to identify anomalies that may signify an incident through automated, continual security monitoring, with manual follow-ups.

Effective security is about managing your risks, monitoring them to make sure they are acceptable and taking appropriate action if not. Importantly, it is not about eliminating all risk and achieving absolute security, as the trade-offs that approach would require – not having an online presence, for instance – are simply too great. However, an acceptable risk is still a risk. Even with a preventive measure in place, that measure might fail, or that measure may have been implemented to only reduce the impact and not necessarily to prevent the risk from materialising. Furthermore, the attacker might be able to circumvent that measure by finding a different way in – after all, a single weakness can be enough to result in a security breach.

This is why it is important for you to take a defence-in-depth approach (discussed in more detail in 12.12.8), and consider measures that make you not just cyber secure, but cyber resilient. Part of being resilient means that you are prepared in the event that your preventive measures fail, because you have combined them with measures to detect and respond to the incident. In other words, detection works where prevention fails (although detection is not very useful if not followed up on – more on response in chapter 14).

For example, if you invest in a fireproof safe, the contents in that safe are not actually protected from fire no matter what. Rather, the safe will be able to withstand a fire for as long as indicated by its fire rating – the higher the rating, the longer the safe's contents will not burn (but the more expensive the safe).[79]

To generalise the safe scenario, a preventive measure may only need to fend off the attack until the response can arrive. This is an important point to take into account as you conduct your risk assessments and decide how to treat an unacceptable risk (also see 12.12.7) – it is not just a case of what your assets might be susceptible to, but also how long they may need to fend off that threat until support can arrive and take control of the situation. To know when to jump into action and minimise the response time, detective measures play a key role.

Detective measures can work at very different times with respect to the event. Not all of them are suitable for every kind of event or attack, but where they do work, they will add a valuable – and often cost-effective – layer of defence. Detective measures can be broadly divided into three types:

1. **Pre-incident detection (prevention):**
   Pre-incident detection involves trying to prevent the attack or event from happening in the first place, by taking appropriate precautions based on information about your environment or industry, or threat

[79] Also bear in mind that a safe suitable for one type of content (e.g. paper documents) may not be suitable for other types (e.g. magnetic media), no matter the fire rating.

intelligence from partners and authorities. In effect, it is a type of prevention – a risk-based approach that allows for a more efficient use of resources. Be conscious, however, that your risks change over time – not just because of the ever-evolving threat landscape, but also because the value of your information will change depending on the circumstances. Information about an upcoming merger or a new product, for instance, is worth a lot more before it reaches the public domain. It is therefore important to periodically conduct or review your pre-incident detection activities to ensure they remain effective.

Concrete activities that fall into this detection category are vulnerability scanning (see 13.1.2) and penetration testing (see 13.1.3), which can identify your vulnerabilities and advise how you might address them before they are maliciously exploited.

2. **Real-time detection:**
   Where you are not able to prevent the attack outright, you want to know, in real time, when you are under attack (whether malicious or otherwise). This might be an alarm going off, a security guard spotting an intruder, an automatically generated notification that someone from an unknown IP address uploaded a file to your web server, etc.

   For cyber security, it is impossible to rely on people to do such proactive, continuous monitoring (and analysis) of all data as it comes in. Without even considering things such as concentration lapses, the amount of data is simply too much, and comes in too rapidly. Instead, you need to rely on automated tools such as intrusion detection systems (IDS) and security information and event management (SIEM) to continuously monitor and interpret the data, and rely on a person to confirm whether any alerts raised really were triggered by an attempted attack, and take appropriate action if necessary.

For physical security, people have a better chance of detecting an (attempted) incident in real time than for cyber security – for example, a security guard watching the live CCTV footage. However, there are still significant limitations to the amount of data they can take in and process at any given time – a single person could not concentrate on more than a few screens, for instance (which is why the primary value of CCTV lies in its ability to build an archive, which can provide vital evidence in the incident response process, discussed in more detail in 14.1.3).

3. **Post-incident detection:**
Unfortunately, most incidents are discovered after the event. In many cases, this can be months or even years later – in 2019, it took an average of 206 days to identify a breach (and another 73 days to contain it).[80] However, if an attacker manages to breach your security despite your best efforts, you still want to know about it, and the sooner, the better, so you can perform damage limitation. If an unauthorised individual only just logged in from an unexpected geographical area, triggering an automated alert to IT, they may not have had a chance

[80] IBM Security, "How much would a data breach cost your business?", July 2019, *https://www.ibm.com/security/data-breach*.

to steal confidential data or elevate their privileges yet. Nonetheless, the fact they managed to get in constitutes a security breach.

Even though this type of detection takes place after an incident has already occurred, it requires careful planning for it to be effective when required. Where do you place your sensors? When an alarm is triggered, who is informed during working hours? What about outside working hours? How will you guarantee that the person(s) appointed will be able to look into the situation on time? These are the kind of questions your risk assessments should answer (see 12.12).

13.1 Threat and vulnerability intelligence

> Receiving intelligence on threats, vulnerabilities and security measures from feeds likely to be relevant to the organisation to keep up with the ever-changing cyber landscape and help inform, in particular, advance and post-incident detection activities.
>
> **Key output:** Following relevant threat bulletins and using them as inputs for your detection activities, as well as a programme of regular vulnerability scanning and penetration testing.

Commanders on the battlefield need to know what is going on before they can make good decisions. For that, they need intelligence. The same principle applies in cyber security: threat and vulnerability intelligence is a key factor in choosing your security measures – after all, you need to know what your threats are before you can effectively defend against them, particularly when resources are limited.

On top of that, the battlefield can see rapid changes, which the commander must be aware of – again, this requires intelligence – and adapt to accordingly. In cyber security, with the ever-changing threat landscape, much the same applies again: you need to keep up with the latest intelligence, and adjust your defences in line with the information you receive. That may mean adding or changing your preventive measures, but might also involve adjusting the configuration on your detective tools or reviewing your logs in a different light to check for missed anomalies. Naturally, it is best to stop the incident from happening in the first place, but if one happens anyway it is better to be aware of the fact belatedly than not at all.

To stay up to date with the latest threats and vulnerabilities, as well as the latest security techniques and solutions, you can do things such as subscribing to weekly threat bulletins, such as the UK NCSC weekly threat reports,[81] the US Cybersecurity and Infrastructure Security Agency (CISA) weekly bulletins[82] and regular bulletins provided by security companies. Regularly checking news websites with a section dedicated to security can also help, as can keeping an eye on the Common Vulnerabilities and Exposures (CVE®) database[83] (which is easiest to do via feeds such as the NIST

---

[81] NCSC, "Weekly threat reports", accessed July 2020, *https://www.ncsc.gov.uk/section/keep-up-to-date/threat-reports*.

[82] CISA, "Bulletins", accessed July 2020, *https://www.us-cert.gov/ncas/bulletins*.

[83] CVE, "CVE Data Feeds", accessed July 2020, *http://cve.mitre.org/cve/data_feeds.html*.

National Vulnerability Database (NVD)[84]). Following forums that provide intelligence likely to be relevant to you based on, for example, industry or vendor, may also be a good idea.

On a less frequent basis, it is also sensible to conduct regular vulnerability scans and penetration tests. This will give you the opportunity to use intelligence from another body – with expert knowledge of how to check for the latest threats and vulnerabilities – without having to internalise that information yourself. In effect, it gives you another pair of experienced eyes to pick up anything you may have missed and check that actions you have already taken have been correctly implemented. Furthermore, any guidance you may receive will be concrete and specific about what and where the vulnerability is, and what to do about it.

13.1.1 Effectively using threat bulletins

Of course, simply receiving notifications of new threats in your inbox every week is not useful in itself. The same is true for going through all bulletins in detail, since that would be a very labour-intensive approach, prone to oversights.

Effective cyber security requires knowledge of the threats you might face. That does not just mean being aware of the latest threats, but also knowing how to identify the threats that might be relevant to you. This requires strong knowledge of your systems and your risk assessments – in other words, knowing what you have within your networks, how your organisation relies on them and how likely a target

---

[84] NIST, "National Vulnerability Database", accessed July 2020, *https://nvd.nist.gov/vuln/data-feeds*.

your systems are based on their inherent weaknesses and how valuable they, or the information they hold, are.

Knowing these things will help you decide what feeds to monitor, and how to filter them effectively. For instance, if your employees rely heavily on mobile phones, you need to keep an eye out for new types of smishing and vishing; if you know that hacktivists may target you, you need to be aware of the details of their latest known campaigns.

Once you have filtered your notifications for (potentially) relevant items, there are two key ways to use that intelligence:

1. **Automated detection tools:**
   Making changes to your tools' configurations or settings based on the information from your feeds so your tools can identify the new anomalies going forward.
2. **Logs:**
   If you know how to recognise activities or behaviours that indicate an attempt to exploit a certain vulnerability you learned about from your feeds, you can manually review your logs from before the alert was sent out to check for those signs. You may also be able to run a new scan or search with an automated tool to retrospectively filter your logs for the new type(s) of anomaly to make the manual follow-up easier. Trying to proactively identify an attacker already in your systems is known as 'threat hunting'.

Using automated tools and logs for general security monitoring activities is discussed in 13.2.

13.1.2 Vulnerability scanning

Vulnerability scanning tools, which are often linked to vulnerability databases such as the CVE, can check for missed patches, unauthorised items, misconfigurations and other possible vulnerabilities. Before you run the automated scans, make sure that you update your tools to the latest versions and databases to be certain that the latest known vulnerability signatures will be used. Where the scanner identifies any weaknesses, it will usually assign a risk rating to the vulnerability based on, for example, the Common Vulnerability Scoring System (CVSS), which you can use to prioritise updates and fixes. Because many tools are linked to a vulnerability database, you will usually also be given or directed to guidance on how to mitigate the weaknesses identified. Be aware, however, that an automated tool can only return a baseline score – it does not take your environment into account, which is a significant factor in determining the true severity of the vulnerability. (A skilled penetration tester, on the other hand, will consider this.)

You should run your scans regularly, at a frequency that makes the window between patch release and scan acceptable to you, and that meets any contractual and other relevant requirements. Bear in mind that such windows vary per software if you rely on a wide range of vendors, as each tends to have a different patch or update cycle.

You may also want to compare the results from consecutive scans to make sure vulnerabilities have been correctly mitigated (some tools do this automatically). It may also be worth assessing the change in the number and significance of vulnerabilities over time – ideally, you will observe a decrease in line with any targets you have set. However, an increase is not automatically cause for concern, as it could be symptomatic of an organisational expansion or a new approach to network development.

13.1.3 Penetration testing

Like vulnerability scanning, penetration testing (also known as ethical hacking) is another form of pre-incident detection. When conducting a penetration test, you have a qualified tester, either on site or remotely, systematically probing your applications, systems and networks to identify any vulnerabilities, giving you the opportunity to remediate them before they can be exploited by someone with malicious intent. It also enables you to focus your security efforts – particularly since the penetration test report(s) should be specific about what and where your vulnerabilities are, and offer recommendations for mitigation – rather than employing broad methods that may require heavy investment without a guarantee that your specific vulnerabilities have been mitigated.

The type of vulnerabilities a penetration test can uncover are more extensive than the ones an automated tool would identify. Experienced penetration testers mimic the techniques used by criminals while ensuring that no damage is caused (and can conduct the tests when networks and applications see the least usage to minimise the impact on everyday operations). This includes using automated vulnerability scanning tools – which criminal hackers also use – to identify not just more clear-cut weaknesses such as unpatched software, but also vulnerabilities that appear harmless on their own but are dangerous when combined. This is the sort of weakness unlikely to be spotted by a casual observer, but criminal hackers deliberately seek out such opportunities.

Different to automated tools, penetration testers also attempt to exploit identified weaknesses as proof of concept (without causing any actual harm to your systems). They may also up- or downgrade the standard risk ratings (automatically assigned by a tool aligned to the CVSS or a similar scoring system) based on, for instance, the sensitivity of the data that could be breached, or because one vulnerability can be exploited to greater effect due to another vulnerability the tester found. It might also be the case that the vulnerability is in practice fairly difficult to access, which is not something a scoring system relying on a necessarily limited number of metrics can always take into account.

As with the vulnerability scans, do not consider a penetration test a one-off activity, but one that should be conducted on a regular basis. You may also need to conduct one in response to an incident to help identify how it happened and what remedial action is necessary, or as confirmation that previous remediation suggestions have been implemented correctly. Penetration testing can also be a contractual obligation if, for example, you are required to comply with the PCI DSS.

Broadly speaking, there are two primary targets for penetration testing, each representing a different aspect of your organisation's logical perimeter:

1. **Network tests:**
   These focus on access to servers and networking devices by probing firewalls, Wi-Fi, etc., looking for holes in the network.
2. **Web application tests:**
   Web applications are often publicly accessible, offering an alternative point of access to your organisation's information. Testing generally (but not exclusively)

focuses on the most common vulnerabilities at the time, such as the Open Web Application Security Project (OWASP) top 10 security risks,[85] checking for SQL injection or cross-site scripting (XSS) opportunities, insecure session management, etc., which an attacker could use to gain access to data or internal systems.

Many organisations have a mix of both, which should be subject to testing, but the methods and results will differ. For network testing, you also need to consider whether you want an external or internal test to be conducted. Each provides a different perspective on how data breaches occur:

1. **External tests:**
   These identify avenues attackers might take in gaining access to your network and systems from an Internet-based perspective.
2. **Internal tests:**
   These look for ways to gain access internally or for an external attacker to elevate their privileges after they manage to gain a foothold on your networks. They also check for information that could be deliberately extracted or accidentally leaked. They can also assess the effectiveness of network segmentation and segregation (also see 12.9.2).

You may also need to look at mobile application testing, wireless (Wi-Fi) testing or build reviews (also known as build and configuration testing). Penetration testing may also

[85] OWASP, "OWASP Top Ten", 2017, https://owasp.org/www-project-top-ten/.

include non-technological testing, such as social engineering and phishing. This could help confirm the effectiveness of your staff awareness training (see 12.11) – or demonstrate that refreshers or visual reminders such as posters may be necessary.

Many organisations start with an external network test, but the most suitable test(s) for you will depend on your requirements. To help establish what solution(s) are best for your organisation's needs, ask questions such as:

- Why are you considering penetration testing? For example, are you trying to meet a contractual requirement, have you set up new offices or launched a new application, or have you recently suffered an incident?
- What do you want to test? This will help determine the scope of your test.
- What is your budget?
- What do you expect to gain from the test? For instance, are you just looking for assurances that your security measures are sound, or are you trying to establish how a recent breach occurred and how you can prevent it from happening again?

Also pay attention to the company carrying out the work – your security testing provider needs to be able to prove that it can be trusted by being, for instance, an accredited member of CREST.[86] If you are testing to meet a specific requirement, such as complying with the PCI DSS, make

---

[86] CREST, "Benefits of using a CREST accredited member company", accessed July 2020, *https://www.crest-approved.org/about-crest/support-to-industry/index.html*.

sure that your chosen company is able to test for specifically that purpose.

13.2 Security monitoring

> The organisation's systems and networks are continually monitored for anomalies, through a combination of automated tools and human input to try to detect incidents as quickly as possible, and continually logged so incidents can be identified and investigated.
>
> **Key output:** Strategically placed sensors that collect data, which is analysed by automated tools in real time, followed up by human input. Collected data is stored so it can serve as evidence in a later investigation if needed.

To reiterate, when you are under attack, you want to know about it immediately (or at least as soon as possible). Likewise, if someone successfully got into your systems, the sooner you knew about it, the sooner you could take action to limit the damage done.

To stand a fighting chance of quickly finding out about an attack, you need to continually monitor and record everything that happens to your systems, networks and premises by generating access and traffic logs, and putting CCTV in place. Doing so will provide you with data you can monitor and analyse to determine what is going on, identify abnormal activity and build an archive you may need later to figure out the exact nature of an incident, which in turn will inform your remediation and recovery activities.

13.2.1 Real-time monitoring

Where you monitor and analyse data in real time to try to identify anomalies quickly, you need to rely on an automated tool, such as a SIEM or an IDS. A human cannot do such digital monitoring, because we are fundamentally limited in the amount of information we can receive and process at a given time, but people nonetheless play a vital role in this process.

A person will be responsible for selecting the tools based on your organisation's needs. The quantity and types of data that the tool would have to analyse in real time, for instance, are major factors. Another point you might want to consider is a reporting capability, which would add a lot of value if your cyber security investments are primarily driven by legal or regulatory requirements.

Furthermore, a person will need to configure your tools in such a way that they can identify anomalies while minimising false positives and avoiding false negatives, taking into account past results and incoming intelligence (see 13.1). After all, an anomaly is simply behaviour deemed out of the ordinary – but the tool needs to be taught, by a human and/or through machine learning, what 'out of the ordinary' means. As discussed in 12.4.7, it could be a specified number of failed login attempts in quick succession, but it might also be things such as a sudden increase in disk usage or suddenly having a lot of free disk space (which could be a sign of ransomware). As another example, you might also want to write a rule that alerts you if a file is uploaded to the web server from an IP address not belonging to your web developers (whose IP addresses have been predefined).

It is also important that complexities such as seasonality are taken into account – particularly in an e-commerce context, for instance, what is considered a normal level of activity at the end of the financial year or on Cyber Monday will be different to what might be normal during school holidays. Teaching the tool to recognise these expected spikes or drops reduces the number of false positives. You may also see a spike while a special offer is ongoing, which could set off false alarms that are harder to anticipate and therefore avoid.

On top of that, your tools only identify and flag anomalies to a human – it is the latter who will have to determine what is really going on, and whether it is an incident, a false alarm or an indication of something else, such as disk space simply running out (in which case you should take action to avoid service unavailability). Furthermore, just knowing that you have been breached is of little use without a follow-up – determining exactly what happened, how it happened and how to contain and remediate the situation.

Ultimately, you want to end up with a 'funnel' where you start off with a lot of collected data relating to specific events, have automated tools filter it for anomalies, which a person then looks at, classifies and escalates as appropriate.

Because the physical security scope to monitor is usually more manageable, humans stand a better chance of spotting an attacker in real time by watching the live CCTV footage. Having said that, it is important not to rely on live human detection alone, as even in a physical environment there are significant limitations, as discussed in the introduction of this chapter. You could rely on AI to detect motion between video frames and alert a person to them, who can then investigate, or simply review the relevant footage if you become aware of a (possible) incident later on – either way,

CCTV's primary value lies in its post-incident detection and evidence-gathering capabilities.

13.2.2 Placing your sensors

For your detective measures to be effective, being strategic about where you place your sensors, and how many you place, is critical. Only relying on sensors outside your firewall would result in non-stop alerts and no specific information – after all, it simply tells you that you are being attacked, which should not come as a surprise. The more useful information lies in whether any of those attacks have been, or are likely to be, successful, and getting that information as quickly as possible, which requires having sensors within your firewall.

Having said that, placing one sensor outside your firewall still has value, as it can inform you of current trends. Suppose, for example, that you are suddenly getting a lot more requests on your VPN server from IP addresses you do not normally connect to and, around the same time, you receive an alert from your IT solution provider saying that it has discovered a vulnerability in its VPN server. Putting two and two together, you can then take concrete action such as patching the software, or deciding that you can manage without that server for a while, and turning it off until a patch is made available.

However, the external threat is not the only thing you need to be concerned about – there is also the danger of the internal threat (discussed in more detail in chapter 8). This could be someone misusing an authorised user's access rights (either the user themselves or by stealing their credentials) or an external attacker who has bypassed your firewall (which creates a tunnel going outside your perimeter, giving the unauthorised user direct access to your internal networks). These dangers have led to the concept of 'zero-trust' architecture, where you do not trust anyone, including those already within your network perimeter (also see 12.9.5). Strong identification and authentication solutions (also see 12.4) are vital to mitigating this risk, as are internal sensors so you can monitor the activities within your networks.

To monitor your internal networks while also getting a sense of the external trends going on, placing your sensors strategically is vital. You should have a sensor as close as possible to where your Internet comes into your building, and another where you have your security appliances (such as firewalls) protecting your networks from unwanted traffic. Placing another sensor on the inside, bypassing your filters, can tell you whether any attacks have been successful. To counter the internal threat, it is also wise to place sensors within your network segments or security zones (also see 12.9.2).

Remember to also consider how many sensors you need: if you have too few, there is a significant risk of missing attacks (and other anomalies); if you have too many sensors, you may be collecting so much data that you risk data overload, and end up with a big bill for processing and storing all that data. Ideally, you want to locate all 'needles' (actionable information) in as small a 'haystack' (data) as possible to optimise your resources without sacrificing security.

13.2.3 Storing data

Keeping logs is a necessary part of security, as most incidents are detected well after the fact, and upon discovery you need to be able to establish what happened in order to be able to effectively remediate the situation. However, it is not realistic to collect lots of data and keep all of it for months or years on end. Since it needs to be stored on servers, keeping a lot of data for a long time can prove expensive, whether you buy a lot of hard drives or pay to store it all in the Cloud.

13.2.2 discussed how the number of sensors you have determines the amount of data you collect. To make strategic decisions about how *long* you retain what data for, think about why you are storing that data. The most straightforward types of data are those subject to regulatory or legal requirements – it is fairly standard, for example, that you are required to keep financial data for seven years. For detection purposes, consider how long it would take you to detect a breach. If the answer is six months (which is not uncommon), keep your logs for at least that long to ensure you have the evidence you need to determine when and what the initial attack was, as well as your recent records that can identify suspicious activities since then to determine the extent of the breach. The logs can also be useful evidence in an audit.

The size of your network will be a significant factor in this decision-making process. If your network is small, it is much more affordable to keep your logs for a longer period (a year, for example). If you have a larger network, you probably have to be more selective about data retention, keeping some for a long time, others for a shorter period, and destroy some data almost immediately. At the end of the day, it is a balancing act between your data retention requirements, including the time needed to detect an incident, and storage cost.

13.2.4 End-user detection

Where a person manages to detect a cyber security incident before an automated tool can pick it up, they are probably the end user rather than the security specialist. An end user might immediately notice that something is wrong because, for example, they see a warning message pop up in their browser (IT might know about an alert from ATP Safe Links, for instance, but not about a warning message in an end user's browser).

To build on that example, if an employee clicked on a link sent to them via email, received an in-browser (not Safe Links) warning and immediately closed down the page, they were stopped from accessing that page, so no incident occurred. Through staff training (see 12.11), that employee should know they must inform IT of the event, if only to confirm that no harm was done. IT might then discover that several more employees received the same email, and send out an all-staff communication to warn them that they may be targeted and generally remind everyone to be vigilant about phishing attacks. Moreover, receiving details on a malicious email that reached end users helps IT review and, if necessary, fine-tune the settings on detective measures to help prevent future malicious links from reaching end users.

It is vital that staff understand their security responsibilities before you can rely on them to report any unusual activity that may or may not be an incident. Whether as mundane as a computer taking much longer than normal to boot up (this could signify a malware infection), or something more obviously abnormal such as a mouse moving of its own accord, staff should be taught – and encouraged – to report such anomalies. Awareness posters, regular training and all-staff communications (particularly in situations such as the one described earlier) can help get that message across and remind staff to be vigilant.

13.2.5 Post-incident detection

Of course, even an effective immediate detection system, with well-configured automated tools and attentive end users, will not be perfect, if only because new threats are constantly emerging. Based on the data coming in and anomalies identified, you may also want to adjust or add to the rules you have set. Furthermore, there can be signs of suspicious activity that an automated tool is unlikely to identify as an anomaly, such as a transaction going to the wrong company, or a larger than normal transaction for that company.

Having said that, automation clearly is a good thing: it filters the data, reducing the problem of receiving more data than a person could handle with any kind of efficiency. Given a smaller, filtered data set and more time (making it post-incident detection), a person will have a much better chance of going through it all and interpreting it with accuracy. It will also give them the time to locate what the automated tool might have missed, whether caused by outdated information, ineffective rules or just outright luck. The person manually reviewing logs might also want to pay attention to signs of ineffective policies, such as internal users accessing information they do not require for their role, which are not necessarily a security incident yet, but could become one if not addressed.

Where an anomaly is identified, your logs (and, for physical security, your CCTV footage) can provide valuable evidence for your incident response process, helping you to determine the origin and full extent of the breach. This evidence gathering and analysis process is discussed further in 14.1.4.

CHAPTER 14: RESPOND AND RECOVER

> To be truly resilient, you need to put responsive measures in place to complete the three-pronged prevention–detection–response system. That way, if an attack succeeds despite your best efforts, you can respond to and recover from it efficiently, prioritising your most critical functions and assets.

We have already discussed that incidents happen no matter how strong your security, and how detection works where prevention fails. That said, even very reliable detection will not do much good if there is no response. Having an effective prevention–detection–response system in place also improves your cyber resilience and is a form of defence in depth (see 12.12.8) – even if one measure fails, other measures will stop the attack from being successful or minimise its impact. You may also find yourself observing sequences such as in the following examples:

Example 1 – logical access

1. **Preventive measure:** password protection.
2. **Detective measure:** access logs show a login from an unexpected geographical area.
3. **More preventive measures**: a second authentication factor (such as an OTP) and segregation.
4. **Responsive measures:** force logout; lock the account; change password; forensics (establish what happened);

consider defence improvements; share information with staff, partners (if they may be targeted too) and regulators (if it was a reportable incident).

Example 2 – physical security

1. **Preventive measure:** physical perimeter – gates, walls, doors, etc.
2. **Detective measure:** (silent) alarms.
3. **More preventive measures:** locked offices, cabinets and drawers; safes.
4. **Responsive measures:** security team arrival, contact the authorities, contact insurance, repair any physical damage.

In both examples, a range of responsive measures came into play, covering several response types. Generally speaking, response measures fall into one of five stages:

1. **Identification:**

   Unless you know that an attack is happening, and know what sort of attack it is, you cannot respond (or respond effectively) to it. The 'identification' stage largely overlaps with the detection processes discussed in detail in chapter 13.

2. **Containment:**

   As soon as you become aware of a (possible) attack, you should look to contain and limit the damage. You can do that either by aiming to stop or delay the attacker – for instance, by forcing logout – or by aiming to reduce the harm to your assets – for example, by locking an account or machine.

Containing an incident is not likely to remove the attacker from your systems altogether, but will buy you time to figure out exactly what is happening and significantly limit the total damage done.

3. **Eradication:**

   Once you have worked out what the attacker has gained access to, what sort of malware you are dealing with, which systems have been affected, etc., you can proceed to eradicate the threat, eliminating every trace of malware and the attacker, and harden and patch your systems. The key is that you eliminate the root cause of the incident and can get ready to restore your systems.

4. **Recovery:**

   Recovery is all about ensuring survival. Now that the threat has been eradicated, you should restore your systems with minimal data loss. This is a process that can happen iteratively (operating at a reduced but acceptable level before recovering in full), and should prioritise the most critical assets and processes. This requires clearly defined recovery goals and, true to the trade-offs inherent to effective security, making sacrifices.

   Preparing for recovery requires advance mitigation – you cannot use sprinklers if you have not installed them or rely on insurance without a policy. However, it also requires clear documentation, including formal procedures and continuity plans, and that staff are familiar with them. Testing your plans regularly (at least twice a year) will help with this; this will also establish whether your plans really work, and give you a chance to improve or correct them if necessary.

5. **Lessons learned:**

   Once you have recovered, you may still be vulnerable to the same attack, particularly if the earlier system hardening and patching did not actually address the cause of this particular incident. It is therefore sensible to reassess the risks, and decide whether and how you need to change or improve your defences. Improvement opportunities identified should be fed into your next continual improvement cycle (see 15.2).

   Also bear in mind that you may have to notify affected parties, including regulators, about the incident if you are required to do so, and that the initial notification may have to be made fairly soon after becoming aware of the incident yourself (the EU GDPR, for instance, requires certain data breaches to be reported within 72 hours of becoming aware of them). Besides the legal requirement, notifying external parties can help them take appropriate precautions before they become a victim too. Making such contributions to the cyber security community improves your organisation's own chances of receiving the same courtesy.

Both immediate and follow-up responses are important. The former will minimise the damage the incident causes, while the latter will ensure your recovery. Your follow-up responses will also limit the impact to your business operations and help you meet your legal obligations, as there are a wide range of laws across the globe that require data breaches to be reported.

When considering what responsive measures to implement, remember that your detection mechanisms may turn up false positives, particularly when automated. Your responsive measures should take this into account – having a process that confirms whether the event was a real (or attempted) attack before taking further responsive action can prove cost-effective, particularly for less reliable detection mechanisms.

Also bear in mind that any responses reliant on people (who in turn usually rely on written plans and procedures) require practice to ensure they can act swiftly when needed. No matter how thought-through your plan, theory is no substitute for practical experience. Testing does not simply confirm that the plan works, but also trains staff to respond as efficiently as possible. At the end of the day, the best response is one that is part of a routine, or one that at least feels familiar. A responsive measure that is not often used (or tested) may give a false sense of security, for in the heat of the moment and in the panic, things probably will not go as planned without practice. Remember that security is a feeling as well as a reality (as discussed in 5.3), and the two do not always converge – this is particularly relevant here. Furthermore, there is always the possibility that a key person is not in the office on the day of an incident, so make sure that a number of people know what to do. This is also a factor that your risk assessment (see 12.12) should account for: you cannot be sure that risks will be faced by a specific person who has appropriate training, so you cannot assume that the risk response will always be the best one.

For instance, in the event of an electrical fire, water extinguishers should not be used – but many people confronted with a fire would instinctively reach for the nearest fire extinguisher. In this example, installing fire extinguishers suitable for fighting fires involving solid combustibles such as paper *and* for fighting electrical fires, such as a foam or water mist extinguisher, can also mitigate the risk. More generally, this type of risk – not being certain that the most suitable person will be faced with the materialised risk – can be partially mitigated with documented and well-communicated instructions.

14.1 Incident response management

In recognition of the risk that your preventive measures can fail no matter how strong, you need to be able to react to and mitigate incidents effectively. To do so, you need to take preparatory steps to have the best chance of making the right decisions when speed is of the essence.

Key output: An incident response team, and clear and tested incident response plans and procedures.

Any kind of management requires sufficient planning and preparation for it to be effective. For incident response management, this requires risk assessment (see 12.12) and putting measures in place appropriate to the risk. As already discussed, such defensive measures can be preventive, detective or responsive.

Clearly, responsive measures are the key focus for incident response management, but remember that these are heavily dependent on the other two categories: detection and prevention. Detective measures play a significant role in deciding when the response should be put into motion, while the more effective the prevention, the less likely you need to rely on your responsive (or detective) measures.

14.1.1 The incident response team

The incident response team is responsible for analysing information about incidents, discussing observations and coordinating activities, and sharing important findings internally. That information typically originates from your detection activities, either as a report from your automated tools, or based on information from an employee, contractor or external party.

The team will also be involved in developing your incident response plans (see 14.1.2), which will be at the heart of your overall incident response management. When not actively investigating suspicious activity or responding to an incident, the team should still meet at least quarterly to review current security trends and incident response procedures.

The team might include a director or senior manager, information security manager, facilities manager and IT manager (some may overlap with the general security team as discussed in 12.10). Whatever the exact roles, the team needs to have the expertise and experience to assess the nature and impact of an incident, and have enough authority to act quickly in response to it. Someone should also have enough awareness of your organisation's legal notification requirements to be able to recognise when an incident might need to be reported, and therefore know when another team (such as the legal or PR team) needs to be informed.

Also bear in mind that if your organisation spans multiple locations, so may an incident. The response team will likely need at least some physical access, if only to reboot a server. As such, it is sensible to strive to have at least one key person in terms of business and/or IT operations, who is also a response team member, at every major location.

14.1.2 Incident response plans

When an incident happens, good decisions have to be made quickly and under pressure. To do so successfully, it is essential to guide employees with written – and tested – incident response plans. These should set out some key information, including:

- Clear objectives and priorities;
- Responsibilities;
- Reporting process/communication plans; and
- Scenario-based checklists or steps.

Your plans should set clear objectives, making your priorities and targets transparent. This means they need to take into account key assets and processes: what are they, how might they be threatened, how big an impact can you tolerate for how long a period, how long can you afford to be without your critical assets and what are your recovery priorities? From there, through workshops and consultations, you can consider the steps and procedures to include in your incident response plans to be able to effectively analyse, mitigate and recover from an incident.

Your plans should also make clear who is responsible for what. Specify the key people, along with their role and contact details, and make sure that at least two people can carry out each task – there is always a risk that someone is absent on a given day. Your plans should also include a reporting process or communication plan to ensure that both incident response team members and relevant stakeholders will be informed of an incident in a timely manner. Such processes should take escalation criteria into account – whoever the incident is escalated and assigned to must be in a position to make critical decisions, including whether and how any relevant authorities should be informed.

Checklists or steps to be taken in the case of specific scenarios may also prove a valuable addition to your incident response plans, ensuring a swift and appropriate response for incidents that can be anticipated. Such scenarios should be developed based on what your most business-critical assets and processes are, as well as your likely threats, and should be identified over the course of a risk assessment. By planning ahead, you will be able to take action without any unnecessary delay, making the development of such scenarios a critical point for your incident response plans.

To be sure that your incident response procedures actually work, you have to test them and document all lessons learned, with improvements incorporated as necessary. Testing at least biannually ensures your procedures are and remain effective, but also enables the documented plan to be as detailed as possible. Also remember that real incidents are relatively rare, but people still need to immediately know what to do if one occurs – for that, training (see 12.10) and tests are essential. On top of that, regular practice will help build and strengthen your organisation's security culture (see 12.11.5).

14.1.3 The incident response process

The exact steps and details of an incident response process will vary depending on an organisation's unique circumstances, but the broad idea is demonstrated in Figure 2. The darker areas represent the 'core' incident response activities; the lighter areas before and after it are detection and the initial investigation, and the follow-up activities respectively.

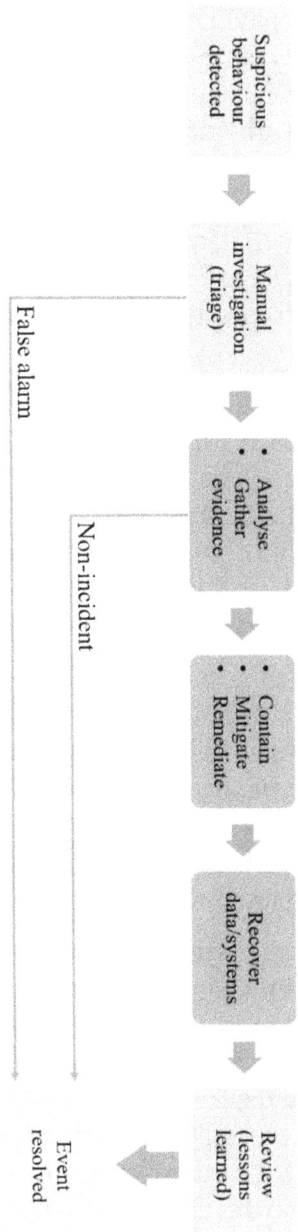

Figure 2: High-level incident response process

Any suspicious behaviour (that could signify an incident) that is detected, whether as an alert from your automated tools or a report from an employee or external party, should be followed up with manual investigation to determine whether it is a false alarm or should be escalated. This triage process must occur as quickly as possible after the initial report. In turn, it will determine the level of urgency if the event must be escalated – can it be dealt with the next day, or do you need someone to drop what they are doing, office hours or not?

Note that escalating the event does not necessarily mean that it was an actual breach – it could still be a non-incident, such as a false alarm or a failed attack. If the latter, you need to check whether the failure was down to your measures working effectively or good fortune (such as a mistake by the attacker). If it was luck, you may still need to take remedial action to prevent future, unluckier occurrences.

Where you escalate the event, you should analyse your data in more detail. This should inform you whether you are really dealing with an incident and, if so, what kind. It should also give you information on how the incident occurred and how severe the impact is or could be, all of which should help you determine what further action to take. Analysis and evidence gathering are discussed in more detail in 14.1.4.

Note that even if the event turns out to be a false alarm or a non-incident, and you can mark the event as resolved, you should still keep a record of it. Occasionally reviewing all records for a given time period can be an informative exercise, indicating that some of your detection mechanisms are not configured correctly and are returning too many false positives as a result, for example. On top of that, such records can demonstrate due diligence in an audit.

After you have remediated the situation – and checked and confirmed that you have really stopped the incident/attacker (this may require a period of monitoring and/or further analysis) – you should look to recover your data and systems, particularly the ones that are vital for resuming business as usual. Recovering and resuming critical business processes as part of BCM is discussed in 14.3.

The final step before marking an incident as resolved is to review your measures and response activities, and consider how they could be improved. Improvement ideas and suggestions should be documented and taken into account in the next cycle of continual improvements (see 15.2).

14.1.4 Analysing and gathering evidence

Some of the first steps to take are fairly basic and can be completed without specialist knowledge. For instance, if an employee reports a suspected incident, or you know which user device the alert came from, you can start asking questions, such as:

- What were they working on and were they connected to the Internet at the time?
- What time did they become aware of the incident, and how long had they been active on the device?
- How did they become aware of the known or suspected incident? For example, a device alert, or realising they clicked a phishing link.
- Have they shared their login credentials with anyone?
- Have they already taken any steps such as contacting someone in IT or shutting down the device?

You should also check what information is stored on or accessible from that device. It is also a good idea to review your access and/or traffic logs to see if you can identify where the incident may have originated from, and if any large quantities of data have been transferred outside your networks. Checking your threat intelligence (see 13.1) may also help identify what type of threat or malware you are dealing with, as well as what you can do to mitigate it. If none of those options have yielded the information you need, you may want to consider hiring a penetration tester to try to identify what caused the incident, and how you can prevent it from happening again (also see 13.1.3).

The classic post-incident scenario starts with an external party telling you that a part of your website, or another public-facing IT asset, has been breached. Since the goal is to understand the details of what actually happened, and not just be aware that an incident occurred, you need clues and evidence. In similar logic to investigating a burglary – where the police would pull the CCTV tapes so they know what the culprit has touched, informing them where they should dust for fingerprints – investigating a cyber security breach starts with checking the relevant logs for the asset you know has been breached. Once you have identified the intruder's IP address, you can use it to check your logs to see what other malicious activities they may have performed. From there, you can work out the full extent and nature of the damage, which in turn guides your containment, mitigation and remediation efforts.

Of course, to be able to conduct such forensic analysis, you need to not just set up security monitoring and logging mechanisms, but also retain those logs long enough to stand a reasonable chance of retracing *all* of the attacker's steps. That said, generating and storing logs of everything for a long time can be financially costly, so it is a matter of assessing the risks and finding the right balance (discussed in more detail in 13.2.3).

It is also important to know whether you are gathering evidence with the intention of using it for internal investigations only, or whether there is any chance of it being submitted as evidence in a court of law. For the latter, clearly, the integrity of the evidence collection process and the evidence itself is critical, so take this into account as you plan and conduct the forensic process.

14.2 ICT continuity management

Business-critical ICT functions should be treated like any other primary business asset, and be resilient in the event of disruption, with risk-appropriate measures put in place to ensure continuity.

Key output: Agreed thresholds and timescales for recovering ICT functions following an incident, along with appropriate fallback measures.

Before addressing business continuity more broadly (see 14.3), it is worth making your ICT services resilient. Most, if not all, modern organisations would not be able to function without their ICT. It is not just a matter of having a large number of IT assets that need to be protected, but also the fact that an organisation often needs its ICT services to manage many of its other continuity activities. For example, backups are an excellent way of protecting your data, but only if you have the systems available to actually restore them.

It is difficult to operate when the delivery of your products and/or services to customers has been disrupted, but impossible to do business if your ICT services are unavailable, particularly for an extended period of time. To ensure that any downtime is minimised, ICT continuity management – preparing for disruptions, so you can quickly recover from a cyber incident – is essential.

ICT recovery management is more than just about preparing your recovery, however. Much like cyber resilience in general, you need to think about prevention first (see chapter 12), as well as considering detection (see chapter 13). Only then should you consider what mitigating and recovering measures, appropriate to the risk, you should put in place. Although you ideally do not want to suffer incidents at all, IT outages unfortunately do happen, whether caused by a malicious actor or accidentally, so knowing how to detect anomalies and quickly do something about them is critical.

Of course, even an efficient recovery will still take time, so make sure you have a fallback of some kind to keep your most critical functions running while the repairs and recoveries are ongoing. When Norsk Hydro suffered its huge ransomware attack in 2019, for example, it was able to keep certain business areas "close to normal despite the attack" by relying on "work-intensive workarounds and manual procedures".[87] It was hardly ideal, but it worked, particularly for a short period. What you certainly do not want is to have no better option than to pay the ransom. This would mean relying on the goodwill of the attacker to actually provide the decryption key *and* not hold onto a copy of the data they

[87] "Cyber-attack on Hydro in brief."

stole, and trusting them not to target you again in a few months. (Ransomware is discussed in more depth in 7.2.3.)

Naturally, since every organisation operates differently, you need to identify what *your* most critical ICT services are, and treat them like any other primary asset. Even if for many organisations this will end up being a relatively short list – such as Internet connectivity, email and website servers, and key databases – the few items on it require as much, if not more, protection as a flagship product or any other primary asset. Segmentation and segregation (see 12.9.2) are valuable controls for protecting the IT estate, since they will prevent a single attack taking out all ICT services at once, and can stop an attacker from taking out your recovery measures too (such as backup servers). You should also agree recovery timescales and thresholds with senior management per critical function. These do not just determine how quick the recovery should take place, but also indicate how effective any temporary IT services need to be, and how long they need to remain functional for.

For smaller organisations that have a limited budget, it can be worth looking into Cloud-based IT services that can be rolled out quickly to take over key functions; for example, providing virtual servers to restore backups to while you clean up the damage. Additionally, if you already make use of Infrastructure as a Service (IaaS) or similar services, your contracts may already include continuity of service, allowing you to pass many of these issues on to the service provider.

Finally, in similar fashion to general incident response procedures (see 14.1), you should document any incidents that have occurred, major or not, so you can review your measures and response, determine what went well and what could be improved, and include any improvement opportunities in your next continual improvement cycle (see 15.2).

14.3 Business continuity management

> Disruptions of varying nature and scale, both foreseeable and unexpected, inevitably occur in business. BCM helps you to prepare for them, ensuring that you can continue to operate – even if at a lower level than normal – no matter what you are faced with.
>
> **Key output:** Business continuity plans, covering multiple broad scenarios, that are based on objective BIA and risk assessment, and have been tested to ensure they work as intended and staff know what is expected of them.

The extreme events of 2020 – when the World Health Organization declared COVID-19 a pandemic and governments around the world intervened at a scale unheard of in peacetime to slow down the spread of the virus – have made organisations look at BCM with fresh eyes.

Although it was probably reasonable not to have planned for pandemics specifically, organisations should have been prepared for more commonplace incidents such as fires and floods, and the consequent unexpected office closures and/or staff being unable to travel.[88] As common as business continuity plans might be, it is almost as common for those

---

[88] This would not have accounted for all problems at the time, of course, such as significantly reduced demand and supply chain issues, but it would have been a good place to start.

plans to be metaphorically (and sometimes literally) gathering dust somewhere – in other words, staff are not familiar with them, so will not know what is expected of them if an incident occurs, and in any case there is no guarantee that those plans will actually work, as they are almost certainly out of date, untested or both.

In any organisational endeavour, a key factor of success is that you can operate without being interrupted by unforeseeable factors – or, for that matter, foreseeable factors. In order to do this, you need to develop an array of contingencies to ensure that resources and productivity are not disrupted by everyday events.

However, everyday events are one thing – significant disruptive incidents, especially at a global scale, are quite another. Most contingencies are developed on an intuitive basis and are intended to deal with short-term problems; when the problems are longer term, or of a scale or nature not anticipated by the designer, they often fall short of what is needed to ensure continued operation, putting the organisation at risk.

BCM is a systematic process of risk management and planning designed to ensure that an organisation can quickly return to an acceptable level of service after a disruption, whatever its nature – be it a cyber attack, organised crime, fire, a pandemic or something else entirely. BCM is about ensuring survival, even in the face of the unexpected, by protecting your organisation's ability to function by ensuring the most critical business functions continue to operate – even if at reduced capacity – while you attend to the disruption.

Because it is impossible to anticipate every single possible type of disruption, organisations must not only rely on their risk assessment, which focuses on what threats might harm them (although this clearly is a valuable part of preparing for the foreseeable). Instead, they should identify their most critical business operations, assets and resources, and consider what backups they can rely on, even if only temporarily.

14.3.1 Business Impact Analysis

In more formal BCM,[89] before you settle on the specifics of your continuity plans, you first conduct a BIA and risk assessment. Although risk assessment is familiar to most managers (the principles of which have been discussed in more detail in 12.12), BIA is a process specifically associated with the field of business continuity. It is also one of the most important processes in BCM.

Unlike risk assessment, where you think about how your assets and business processes may be affected and what the overall severity of a given risk scenario might be, in a BIA you assume your business activities have been disrupted – no matter what by – and think about how you will carry on and recover within an acceptable time frame.

There are typically six steps in a formal BIA, which are outlined below. Organisations that only want a basic level of business continuity arrangements will not need to go into quite this level of detail, and for many of them, a simpler approach will work just fine. Nonetheless, they may find it useful to at least read the six steps and familiarise themselves

[89] See 29.1 for a more detailed discussion on formal BCM, in line with international standard ISO 22301.

with the principles of assessing business impact consistently and reliably before deciding what approach to use.

1. **Identify key activities and resources:**
   What do you need to ensure the continuity of? What resources are required to achieve that continuity?
2. **Establish impact criteria:**
   Similar to criteria/levels for measuring impact and likelihood in a risk assessment, it is simplest to present your business impact criteria in a table format to ensure your chosen criteria are applied consistently across the organisation. If possible, align your criteria to different types of damage, such as financial impact, reputational impact, etc. In similar thinking to risk tolerance, consider the point at which the impact becomes unacceptable to your organisation.
3. **Determine the impact over time:**
   At what point in time does the business impact of having your key activities/resources disrupted become measurable, and at what time intervals does the impact significantly change? Plot these points on a timeline – this will help you determine the order and speed of recovery.
4. **Establish points of unacceptable impact:**
   Now that you have established impact criteria, the impact over time and what impact level is unacceptable, you can decide what your maximum tolerable periods of downtime and recovery time objectives should be. For information systems, take recovery point objectives (RPOs) into account – these describe the minimum level

of information necessary for an activity to resume, which in turn informs decisions on, for example, backup frequency.

5. **Determine recovery priorities:**
   Use the recovery time objectives established in step 4 for this, and remember to take budget restraints into account.
6. **Feed outputs into the recovery strategy:**
   Now that you have consistently and objectively determined your recovery priorities, use that information to draft your continuity plans.

Much of the thinking behind these steps reflects many of the themes discussed throughout this book. Start by determining what your most important assets (or, in this case, business processes) are, then choose a method for consistent measurement of impact so you can effectively prioritise and optimise the use of resource. Ultimately, your analysis and assessments should be fed into your business continuity plans and inform your overall recovery strategy.

14.3.2 Business continuity plans

As highlighted before, business continuity plans are probably the most common continuity management aspect that organisations tend to have, but they are often not as valuable or effective as they should be.

When developing your continuity plans, do not try to develop a plan that accounts for all possible scenarios. Such a plan will be unwieldy, needlessly complex and prone to failure, not to mention that you probably cannot foresee absolutely every kind of disruption. Instead, develop several broad scenarios for which responses are likely to be similar. You might, for example, develop plans for the following:

- Major site or premises incidents (fires, floods, etc.);
- Information and communications system failures (whatever the cause);
- Supply chain failures; and
- Pandemics and similar scenarios.

Approaching continuity plans in this manner allows appointed staff to focus on responses to those scenarios, saving time, money and effort.

Plans should be clear and specific, and directly refer to the predefined thresholds for activating the plan. They should also set out when the plans can be deactivated, how reporting is conducted, the roles and responsibilities of people involved in deploying the plan, and any supporting information necessary. The plans should also be accessible to all those who will need to use them when activated, so be sure to communicate them effectively to whoever needs to know what is expected of them. As is typical of general incident response activities, it is also sensible to keep an incident log to inform your continual improvement activities (see 15.2) and improve future responses.

You should not wait for an incident to happen before you first activate your plan, however. Instead, conduct exercises once or twice a year, and record and evaluate the outcome to identify any issues or deficiencies, and use them as inputs for your improvement activities. Besides making sure that your plans actually work as intended, it will also help familiarise staff with what they need to do. Exercises are, as an activity in itself, a means of mitigating the risk and making your business more secure. Real incidents should be rare, but that is not an excuse for being unable to act swiftly when the time comes.

CHAPTER 15: GOVERN AND ASSURE

> Validate your security efforts, make corrections and improvements where possible, and ensure ongoing board-level oversight of and commitment to cyber security.

The final CRF control category, 'govern and assure', comprises activities that ensure and demonstrate an ongoing and organisation-wide commitment to security. Governance is about ensuring the project is suitably overseen, and assurance is about providing evidence to the oversight authority (both internal and external, where necessary) so they can make sensible, reasoned decisions about it. More concretely, that might mean making your chosen cyber security processes part of a larger structure, with clear governance lines (see 15.4) and visible board-level support (see 15.3), in a formal security programme (see 15.1).

The governance lines should make cyber security responsibilities and accountability clear, perhaps by organising different elements of the CRF into functions overseen by an accountable director or steering committee, while board-level support is essential for securing resources and enforcing a security culture among employees. Ultimately, people are a vital element of security, and if the board does not appear to take security seriously, employees will, unfortunately, follow suit.

Of course, strong communication is a prerequisite to make any kind of formal programme a success: the person managing it needs to be able to explain progress and activities to the board, while staff need to understand what is expected of them, whether they are given specific security-related responsibilities or just need to remain cautious when doing anything online or processing confidential data.

Another useful means of demonstrating your commitment while validating that measures are working as intended are regular internal audits (see 15.5) and potentially external certification (see 15.6). Conducting regular audits will also help the person managing the overall security programme present evidence to the board that the actions already taken have been effective, while seeking certification can help prove both your organisation's commitment to and the effectiveness of your security to external stakeholders, including customers and regulators.

Furthermore, internal audits can highlight where there is room for improvement to ensure your security measures are as effective as possible, and remain up to date and adequate for your needs – after all, not only does the cyber landscape frequently change and evolve, but your operations are also likely to change over time, whether in the form of entering a new market, an infrastructure change, new regulatory requirements or something else entirely. Corrective actions from audit reports, user feedback, performance monitoring, etc. can all be useful inputs for your improvement initiatives, which you should conduct on a cyclical basis as part of your continual improvement process (see 15.2).

All these 'govern and assure' activities add value to any cyber security programme, but are also an essential characteristic of mature programmes. Every activity discussed in this chapter contributes to sustaining your commitment to security across the organisation, whether to demonstrate results, find ways to improve, or both.

15.1 Formal information security management programme

This metaprocess, binding together and unifying the other CRF processes, entails a structured approach to securing information assets across the organisation, taking people, processes and technologies into account. As you establish the processes and implement controls, you should also decide how you will measure and monitor their performance to validate their effectiveness.

Key output: A clear management structure; defined scope; roles and responsibilities; documented policies and procedures; and a strategy for measurement.

An information security management programme is a structured approach to information and cyber security, appreciating that effective security requires a set of activities to work together in harmony in order to protect your information assets and systems. The programme should formalise these activities, as well as relevant structures, roles and responsibilities, in appropriate documentation (see 15.1.1). The programme should also recognise that it is necessary to measure and monitor the performance of those activities to determine whether they are effective (see 15.1.2).

You can establish the formal security programme at the beginning of your project, which will help give structure to your implementation, but you might also choose to first establish the desired practices gradually, and have a good idea of who is responsible for what, before making them all part of a formal programme that:

- Has a clear management structure;
- Clarifies scope, roles, responsibilities and accountability; and
- Has all the necessary documentation, including policies, procedures and records.

These elements will not just help your security-related activities work more in harmony, but also help strengthen your security culture (see 12.11.5). It will also help you produce evidence that you may need for an audit or investigation, and validate for yourself that your processes are functioning effectively.

15.1.1 Creating effective policies and procedures

It is not easy to know where to begin when creating a new policy or procedure (or overhauling an existing one), but a good place to start is to understand the distinctions and how they are linked.

Policies are normally documents that provide a high-level overview of your organisation's aspirations in relation to matters that fall within the policy's scope. As an example, your main information security policy (see 12.2.1) should clearly state where the organisation wants to be from a security perspective, and set out or link to your security objectives. A policy describes your approach to the subject in broad terms, outlines the scope (and any relevant goals or objectives, where appropriate), and makes clear who is responsible for approving, reviewing and updating it when necessary.

Clearly, policies have benefits. They can effectively communicate the organisation's position on a given matter to all staff and contractors, as well as any external stakeholders, which can help them make decisions about how to act in situations not specifically covered by a defined process or procedure. They are also a good way for security professionals to describe the value of security to the board, senior management and any other stakeholders. Last but not least, they are also a good tool for the board or senior management to demonstrate their commitment and leadership to the process.

However, policies can also have serious limitations if they have not been well designed. They can be too complex or vague, making them difficult to understand, which commonly leads to the policy being ignored. Staff might also not follow the policy if it has not been communicated properly, meaning that they forget about it or may even not realise it exists.

From your policies, you derive further documentation, such as procedures and records. Procedures set out how the policy is put into practice in specific areas. The main body of procedures are typically step-by-step instructions for performing a specific task, while records are produced when a procedure is followed, such as a checklist showing that a workstation has been set up and cleared for use, or an automated log showing that a network has been scanned for malware. Procedures should be clear enough that whoever needs to use them can easily understand who is responsible for carrying out each element and how, and what records will be generated. As such, they should be developed by someone close to the process itself – for instance, someone in the IT team would develop a procedure for setting up a workstation, while the facilities manager might develop the procedure for changing the key code on the front door.

Procedures can be very helpful for instructing and guiding employees in doing specific tasks, provided that they are clear. Just like policies, poorly designed procedures will not be followed or will be ignored altogether, which can lead to staff taking an unstructured, ad hoc approach.

As you start drafting the policy- or procedure-specific details, there are a few key points to bear in mind to help ensure they will be effective:

- **Keep your policies and procedures realistic** – policies, of course, need to be aspirational, and procedures need to instruct – the idea of one is that it says where you want to be, while the other guides employees in more specific tasks. Both can influence or even change staff behaviour, but they should also be practicable – if they look like an overly idealised version of the situation, they are unlikely to be effective, as staff will feel they are not realistic or reasonable and will probably end up ignoring them.
- **Keep your procedures as clear and straightforward as possible** – even if your intent is realistic, if your procedures are difficult to follow, either because they have not been written clearly enough or make a straightforward idea seem too complicated, staff will not find them helpful, which will again result in your procedures being ignored or not followed as intended.
- **For procedures, get and incorporate input from the people required to follow them** – although someone in

a managerial position can provide insight into how they would like things to be done and can set targets, that person does not necessarily oversee day-to-day tasks, meaning that they may not be fully aware of typical approaches or challenges. Alternatively, if management insists on a particular method or target, the operational-level employees may be able to suggest what resource changes will be necessary to achieve it. Talking to multiple people working at operational level will help keep your procedures realistic and easy to enforce.

- **Avoid duplication** – in the same way that our CRF has process overlaps, so will the documentation within a given organisation. Consider where one procedure may interact with another, and make sure that they do not cover the same point in the same way. If you do discover this, eliminate them by, for example, just keeping that section in document A and replacing it in document B with a reference to document A. This avoids wasted effort, and also prevents the possibility of that process only getting updated in one of the two documents, potentially causing confusion further down the line. Bear in mind that all documentation should have a document control section for tracking changes.
- **Regularly review and update your documentation** – procedures almost always evolve with time, so should be regularly reviewed and, where necessary, updated. Policies may need to change over time, although not as much as procedures, so require less frequent reviews. In both cases, each policy or procedure should specify the

role that is responsible for maintaining that particular document. That person should therefore also ensure the procedure (or policy) is regularly reviewed to keep it in line with business and regulatory requirements.

Apart from regular reviews (ideally at least annually), it is also important to encourage staff – particularly those who are relatively new and are therefore more likely to bring valuable fresh perspectives – to challenge the status quo where appropriate and suggest improvements.

15.1.2 Measurement

Even assuming that you start your implementation project with good intentions and make good decisions on what measures to implement, any project can peter out without visible, clear results, particularly if this leads to reduced resources.

Unfortunately, it is not easy to measure the effectiveness of security – unless it has failed. The lack of quantifiable metrics can make it challenging to justify to the board and senior management that the measures you have implemented are effective. Nonetheless, there are ways of presenting clear results, including but not limited to:

- Presenting risk assessment results, showing risk levels before and after risk treatment (also see 12.12);
- Comparing the results of consecutive vulnerability scans to assess the change in the number and significance of vulnerabilities over time (also see 13.1.2);

- Penetration testing reports (also see 13.1.3) to show, for example, that:
    - An 'attacker', particularly one relying on automated tools, has no easy way of getting in;
    - Vulnerabilities have been effectively remediated (with consecutive tests); or
    - Staff awareness training has been effective (with a simulated social engineering test).
- Incident response exercise reports (also see 14.1.2), indicating whether target times – potentially influenced by legal breach notification requirements – are being met; and
- Monitoring your network for attack attempts (also see 13.2) – detecting a high number of unsuccessful attacks is a sign that both your detective measures (they are detecting attacks) and preventive measures (attacks are not succeeding) are correctly implemented.

However you intend to approach measurement, you should decide your methods as you select your controls. It is also important to have a baseline – which can be qualitative or quantitative, depending on the control – to allow for clear comparison. You should also have a clear idea of your targets, objectives and requirements, which will help interpret the measurement results, highlighting areas with strong performance and opportunities for improvement.

Finally, bear in mind that there is no need to measure absolutely everything in order to get meaningful results and see a clear return on investment. Prioritise the controls that are intended to mitigate the biggest risks directly related to your objectives, most likely to fail, and the most expensive to implement, maintain and/or repair.

Measurement is discussed further in step 8 of our eight-step approach to implementing cyber security (see chapter 25).

15.2 Continual improvement process

> Security measures should be regularly reviewed, and improved or adapted where necessary, in a continual, cyclical improvement process.
>
> **Key output:** Formal review and planning stages for existing processes, preferably in addition to a formal 'lessons learned' process. Some organisations may also want to adopt a more widespread improvement model, or extend one already used to include cyber security.

Continual improvement should be a key and frequent part of any organisation's operations, whether with a view to improving product quality, process efficiency, cost cutting or anything else that can help improve the way your organisation does business and operates. A continual improvement process, however, is about much more than just the general efforts businesses make to improve their resilience or profitability. This is particularly true in a cyber security context.

Organisational cyber security strategies are, often for very good reason, prone to change – for example, when the threat landscape has changed. However, your cyber security requirements can also change for other reasons – for instance, if you need to pass a security audit in order to win a big contract, or if a new security law comes into effect.

Equally, there can be unexpected situations in which you may be forced to adapt and innovate, which in turn can require an update to your cyber security strategy. A particularly extreme example of this was the global response to the COVID-19 pandemic, which required people all over the world to stay at home and many businesses to let staff work remotely. From a cyber security perspective, this required quick action to ensure people could work securely from home, and potentially from their personal devices – both points inherently less secure than an office network and environment.

When your cyber security strategy, objectives and/or requirements change, having a continual improvement process in place can help you carry through the necessary adaptations and changes. For more ongoing changes, such as adapting to the threat landscape, having a cyclical, continual improvement process in place means that you can make regular, small changes, and significantly mitigate the risk of incurring a large cost if you suddenly need to make big changes to catch up.

A formal, continual improvement process, in which you keep changes small but frequent, is also an excellent way of gradually developing your cyber defences into something more mature, while keeping your implementation project manageable. This is discussed more in step 5 of our eight-step approach (see chapter 22).

15.2.1 Inputs for improvement initiatives

Improvement ideas and suggestions can come from anyone, including but not limited to staff, customers, partners, suppliers, regulators and auditors. Inputs for improvement initiatives can also originate from reviews, audits, 'lessons learned' activities, corrective actions, etc.

Crucially, it is important not to solely rely on people taking the initiative and other ad hoc ways of getting inputs. A 'suggestions box' cannot hurt, but to keep improvement continual and manageable, consistency is key. This means incorporating continual improvement activities into your existing processes – if reviews and planning stages become business as usual, with improvement opportunities identified and implemented as part of that, you are well on your way to achieving the cyclical continual improvement process you should be aiming at.

15.2.2 Implementing a continual improvement process

If your organisation already uses a continual improvement methodology, it is easiest to just extend it to include cyber security initiatives. However, if no formal process exists, it probably makes more sense to apply continual improvement principles to existing processes, and later look to adopt a formal, continual improvement model (two of which are discussed in 15.2.3 and 15.2.4).

You could do this by, for example, introducing formal review stages to a process, such as evaluating projects at completion and two months after completion – did the project achieve its intended goals? Was it completed on time and within budget? Answering such questions – and where the response is negative, determining where things went wrong and how to prevent the same mistake from happening again – and following up with the necessary changes should improve the odds of success for future projects. Alternatively, if everything happened as it should, such a review allows you to conclusively determine that the project truly was a success, which in turn suggests little should be changed for future projects.

Existing processes will also benefit from incorporating formal planning stages, which should take feedback from past reviews (and audits) into account, ensuring improvements are not just suggested, but also implemented. Equally, if the review found that little needed to be changed, this will allow you to complete the planning stage of a new project quickly and confidently.

It is also sensible to have a 'lessons learned' process, where feedback and responses from all reviews over a given period are looked at together to identify patterns or trends, which can in turn lead to new improvement initiatives.

15.2.3 Plan-Do-Check-Act (PDCA) cycle

One very widely used continual improvement methodology is the PDCA cycle or model, visualised in Figure 3. This provides an iterative process for continual improvement to take place, and tends to form the basis of many management systems.

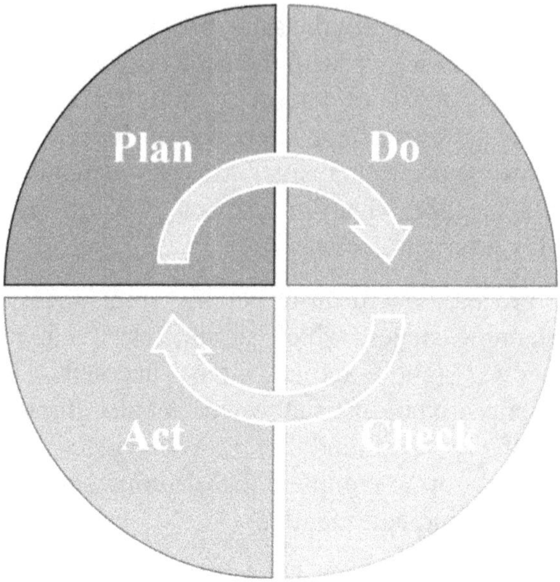

Figure 3: Basic visualisation of the PDCA cycle

The idea is that you first establish exactly what it is you intend to do (**Plan**) – what objectives and processes are necessary to stay in line with your policy? Do you need to make changes based on feedback from the previous cycle?

Next, you execute what you planned (**Do**), followed by monitoring and measuring the outputs against the benchmark (**Check**; see 15.1.2 for more on measurement). The measurement outcomes should be reported and reviewed, from which you can take any corrective actions necessary (**Act**), thus continually improving.

15.2.4 ITIL® 4's continual improvement model

The continual improvement model from ITIL 4, a popular IT service management (ITSM) framework, consists of more steps than the PDCA cycle, but differs fundamentally very little. This model is a high-level, seven-step cycle designed to help organisations establish their current and target positions from an ITSM perspective (though you can extend it to other parts of the organisation too). It also helps organisations plan how they will achieve their target, and how they will embed successful changes (or learn from failed initiatives).

The seven steps are as follows:

1. **Define the initiative's vision:**
   This will help with subsequent decisions, and link actions to the organisation's overall goals and objectives.
2. **Understand your starting point:**
   In order to track and understand your improvement, you need to know where you started from – assess the current state of your products, services, etc. from various aspects, preferably through objective measurement that can also be used in step 6.
3. **Outline what your destination should look like:**
   It is also important to define your target. Remember that your target does not need to fully realise your vision, just progress towards it, and that it is aspirational. In other words, bear in mind that the goal is to improve, not to achieve perfection. (This is worth remembering no matter what methodology you use!)
4. **Plan the journey:**
   If the destination requires only a small change from the starting point, the journey should be direct and straightforward. If more complex changes are

necessary, it may be worth breaking up the work into smaller efforts and evaluating progress, with a possible change of direction, after each iteration.

5. **Execute the plan:**
   Take the planned action, but remember to keep an open mind – particularly if the work is broken up into smaller efforts, you may need to change direction in order to reach the intended destination.
6. **Check that you have reached your desired destination:**
   Check and confirm what progress has been made (ideally with the same, objective measurement mechanism you used in step 2), and that what you have achieved still has value (after all, factors such as customer expectations may change). If one or both are not the case, you may need to take additional action.
7. **Embed the changes in the organisation:**
   To keep the momentum going, and prevent any improvements from being reversed, promote your successes and reinforce any new methods. Should the initiative have failed, analyse what went wrong, and document and communicate the lessons learned, thereby improving the chances of the next iteration's success.

Step 7 feeds back into step 1, restarting the cycle. Note that the model is flexible – organisations are not expected to rigorously follow these steps, but adjust them in line with their culture and goals in a way that ensures their projects' success rates improve.[90]

15.3 Board-level commitment and involvement

> Considering that cyber security is an increasingly important prerequisite for doing business, the potential impact of breaches and the need for a top-down approach to make the cyber security implementation project successful, the board and/or top management should take an active – and visible – interest in cyber security.
>
> **Key output:** The board and/or top management visibly takes cyber security seriously by allocating sufficient resources and, where necessary, offering direction and support to cyber security efforts.

According to a 2020 study by Ernst & Young, only 54% of organisations regularly schedule cyber security as an agenda item for board meetings, and even fewer organisations (40%) have a head of cyber security at board or executive management level.[91]

---

[90] ITIL® is a registered trade mark of AXELOS Limited. All rights reserved. For more information about ITIL 4, see ITGP's publication *ITIL® 4 Essentials – Your essential guide for the ITIL 4 Foundation exam and beyond, second edition*: https://www.itgovernancepublishing.co.uk/product/itil-4-essentials-your-essential-guide-for-the-itil-4-foundation-exam-and-beyond-second-edition.

[91] "EY Global Information Security Survey 2020."

In the past, cyber security was thought of as primarily an issue for the IT department. In a world where technology forms an integral part of the business, however, ensuring that technology works as it should is part of an organisation's strategy, and as such is a matter for the board. How well an organisation delivers its IT services both internally and externally directly impacts how satisfied customers are, and therefore overall business success.

In fact, having a reputation for reliable and secure services can help an organisation stand out from the competition, and be an active means of generating revenue. A 2019 study found that, particularly after a bad experience, consumers are willing to pay a 10–30% premium on the base price of an IoT device for the peace of mind that their privacy would be protected.[92] Being able to show a clear commitment to cyber security is also an increasingly common prerequisite for winning new business, particularly government contracts.

Moreover, the possible impact and cost of a cyber incident is now more severe than ever. There is not just a growing body of legislation under which organisations could face hefty fines – most notably the EU GDPR – but data breaches and cyber attacks also tend to receive more media coverage now. In turn, this can lead to significant financial and reputational damage in the form of, for example, service unavailability,

---

[92] Emami-Naeini, Pardis, et al., "Exploring How Privacy and Security Factor into IoT Device Purchase Behavior", May 2019, *Proceedings of the 2019 CHI Conference on Human Factors in Computing Systems*, *https://dl.acm.org/doi/10.1145/3290605.3300764*.

lost customers and contracts, reduced share prices and loss of competitive edge.

15.3.1 Securing board commitment

It is vital that you secure the board's and senior management's commitment to any cyber security project, as without this, implementation will fail through a combination of insufficient resources and a lack of organisation-wide commitment – if staff cannot see top management taking security seriously, it is unlikely that they will either.

With the possible impact of a breach so significant, it can be tempting to try to convince management with shock tactics by simply citing real-life incidents experienced by partners and competitors. If you do use these, take care to use them in moderation as they can often appear to managers to be extreme and unlikely scenarios, and can cause them to simply switch off. Rather than over-focusing on these incidents, you should focus clearly on the fact that cyber security is an increasingly important prerequisite to compete for business, and that their visible support is essential to the long-term success of any cyber security programme. If staff can see that management are taking security seriously, they are much more likely to take note too – this is crucial to building an organisational security culture (also see 12.11.5).

It may also be worth reminding directors that they have a duty under Section 172 (1) of the UK Companies Act 2006 (and equivalent laws in other jurisdictions) to consider "the likely consequences of any decision in the long term", and "the desirability of the company maintaining a reputation for high standards of business conduct".

15.3.2 Demonstrating board support

There are different ways in which the board can show its commitment to cyber security, although the two primary ones tend to be providing appropriate resources to implement and maintain security, and directing and supporting people. The latter, however, can manifest itself in very different ways depending on the organisation; for instance, senior management might:

- Set relevant objectives and integrate them into business processes;
- Sign off information security policies (see 12.2);
- Visibly adhere to security best practice themselves, and welcome challenges if someone thinks improvements can be made;
- Give regular briefings on the importance of cyber security and the steps the organisation is taking;
- Provide a keynote address or introduction to cyber security training materials;
- Identify possible barriers to implementation by talking to operational-level managers about their concerns, and finding ways to overcome those barriers; and
- Review internal audit findings (see 15.5) and suggest improvements (see 15.2).

Remember that the key is to be *visibly* adhering to company policies, promoting best practices, supporting lower-level staff, etc. If the board only guides from behind closed doors or delegates its responsibilities to others, many of the benefits of board support will be lost or not realised to their full potential.

Where the board is generally not the hands-on type, top management should be taking the responsibility of showing top-level support for cyber security, and guide and support where necessary.

15.4 Governance structure and processes

> As the effectiveness and reliability of an organisation's IT products and services are usually of clear strategic importance to an organisation's ability to do business, intellectual capital and ICT should be overseen by its governing body.
>
> **Key output:** Identified directors are accountable for the delivery of the organisation's IT products and services, and regularly evaluate, direct and monitor IT-related activities.

General corporate governance duties and principles, such as setting out strategic aims, monitoring performance and communicating with shareholders, are widely known and exercised. It is less common, however, to see those principles extended to an IT context. Yet, they should be. IT is not merely a functional or operational issue – intellectual capital and ICT are of clear strategic importance to the vast majority of organisations. Having them inefficient or outright compromised will impact the organisation's ability to do business – the only question is how badly.

15.4.1 Core IT governance practices

Crucially, directors (or a steering committee) should:

- **Evaluate** the current and future use of IT, as well as the effectiveness of cyber security measures, on a regular basis – this includes strategies, implementation plans, supply arrangements, etc., and should take external pressures such as technological change, the threat landscape, economic and other trends, and the political climate into account;

- **Direct** by assigning responsibilities to management and the CISO for implementing IT and cyber security plans and policies. Directors should also ensure that they are kept up to date, so they are in a position to ensure that IT and cyber security projects move smoothly into the operational phase, significantly improving the chances of success; and
- **Monitor** the performance of IT- and cyber security-related activities, ideally through a combination of updates from management and internal audits (see 15.5), in such a way that directors receive information in a timely manner, allowing them to act quickly if there are any problems.

It is important to remember that even where actions are delegated, ultimately the accountability for effectively, efficiently and securely delivering IT services remains with the board. There are also best-practice principles to follow, which will help guide good decision-making in terms of IT governance:

1. **Responsibility** – the persons with IT- and cyber security-related responsibilities must also have the authority to perform the activities they are responsible for.
2. **Strategy** – the organisation's overall business strategy should take into account current and future IT

capabilities, and the IT and cyber security strategies should take business requirements into account.

3. **Acquisition** – decisions on IT and security investments should be clear and transparent, balancing cost and opportunity, with a clear understanding of short- and long-term risks.
4. **Performance** – IT products and services, and cyber and information security measures, should be fit for purpose.
5. **Conformance** – IT assets and processes should comply with all applicable legal and contractual requirements, including from a security perspective.
6. **Human behaviour** – IT and security policies, practices and decisions should respect human behaviour.

15.5 Internal audit

The organisation's information security measures are independently reviewed for their effectiveness on a regular basis, providing the assurance that they are fit for purpose and working correctly. The audit results are reviewed and assessed by senior management.

Key output: A programme of regular internal audits, conducted objectively by an impartial auditor, with results reported to management.

An internal audit is an effective means of independently verifying an organisation's security measures, and an essential element of any continual improvement regime (see 15.2). In some cases, it can also be a contractual or legal requirement, although conducting regular audits is a valuable activity in its own right.

An auditor should check for points such as:

- Is appropriate documentation in place, including policies, processes, procedures and records (also see 15.1.1)?
- Do policies, processes and procedures reflect the reality, and are they being used correctly (or at all)?
- Have appropriate risk assessments been conducted (see 12.12), and is there evidence that all risk responses have been correctly implemented?
- Have implemented controls been checked and measured for effectiveness? Are measurement trends positive?
- Have relevant legal, regulatory, contractual and business requirements been met?
- Have actions and opportunities for improvement from previous audits been documented and pursued?

15.5.1 Impartiality and objectivity

For an audit to be valuable, the auditor must be as impartial and objective as possible. Even if the organisation being audited employs the auditor, which inevitably limits their independence, they should at least be independent of the process being audited. In other words, they should not audit processes for which they are wholly or partially responsible themselves – having someone review their own work or documentation is not a recipe for impartiality.

A larger organisation can avoid this by having a dedicated auditor or audit team; a smaller company could assign the role to two people, and have the second person audit the processes that the primary auditor has some sort of vested interest in, so all processes can be assessed without bias or conflicts of interest. Alternatively, smaller organisations could benefit from outsourcing (see 12.13.2 for SLA considerations). It guarantees impartiality, can give access to better expertise and may reduce cost, and may also improve receptiveness to the audit findings (it is generally easier to listen to criticism from an unquestionably independent, external party specifically brought in to conduct the audit than from someone who might be suspected of having a personal agenda (whether true or not)).

Aside from impartiality, the other key characteristic of an audit is objectivity. For this, evidence is essential. Without it, you would expect some supposition, conjecture or assumption. The amount of evidence required for a functional audit depends on the type of audit and the function being audited, but it is usually sufficient for the auditor to see that evidence and then record the fact in their report – the evidence itself need not be recorded. The report should, however, consist of factual and objective statements such as 'five IT processes were found to be out of date' or 'the incident reporting process is not being followed because it no longer reflects changes to the system that were introduced on 1 August 2019, as stated during interview with auditee'.[93] Supposition and conjecture have no place in such reports.

---

[93] As a general rule, it is wise to avoid naming names in an audit report where possible to reduce the risk of retribution (conscious or otherwise). Even though managers at all levels should understand that punishing employees for telling the truth in an audit does more harm than good, and goes against building the healthy security culture discussed in 12.11.5, being able to guarantee to interviewees that they will not be punished for honesty ensures the most trustworthy and valuable results.

15.5.2 The auditing process

Many auditors start by asking to see your documentation, including policies, procedures and records, since these indicate what *should* happen. The auditor then checks through, or has the auditee demonstrate, the process in question to see if what really happens matches up with what the documentation states; any discrepancies are noted as nonconformities.

Another common way to start an audit is with interviews: an auditor may ask the auditee to talk them through the process, which can highlight significant discrepancies before they even move to checking any documentation.

Either way, note that auditing is always based on sampling – it is not possible to check everything. As useful as audits are, they are still, to some extent, a process dependent on chance. Auditing a particular organisation on a particular day may turn up multiple nonconformities, or none at all, depending on the activities being performed that day. As such, the absence of nonconformities in a given audit does not mean that they do not exist. Good audit performance, even over a longer period of time, should not be used as an excuse to relax the measures that made for good audit performance in the first place.

For consistency and to reduce the risk of missing anything, particularly for detailed audits, auditors can prepare checklists, which can be based on the organisation's implementation plan, risk assessment or list of processing activities. Any of them can be suitable, as long as there is an effective means of prioritising high-risk or high-impact areas; otherwise, the audit is in danger of becoming a box-ticking exercise that serves little practical purpose. Auditors can also prepare a checklist based on best-practice guidance issued by, for example, the NCSC or ICO, or a particular regulation or management system standard.

However, checklists also have disadvantages, primarily because they can be artificially limiting. An auditor who sticks to their checklist religiously may miss opportunities to delve deeper into the root of issues they encounter. One who does not rely on a checklist as strongly or at all will find it easier to take the time to investigate something in depth during an audit, rather than note their initial observation and move on. Not having this flexibility can be a serious drawback, as identified nonconformities should be followed to the root cause, even if that takes time and/or leads to other areas of the business.

Also be aware that even audits that do not rely on a checklist prepared in advance must be conducted against *something* – after all, a nonconformity is something that is not compliant with some sort of requirement. Whether it is a specific regulation or the organisation's list of processing activities, there has to be some sort of base or requirement set against which to identify a nonconformity or, for that matter, prepare a checklist. With experience, auditors will learn what to look for, particularly within an organisation they are already familiar with, since they will know where the key points of failure are.

Where a nonconformity has been recorded, a corrective action must be issued to mitigate it. Where the nonconformity is an open-and-shut case, the auditor should be able to define the corrective action themselves. However, in many instances, the auditee needs to provide input, since they often have the clearest idea of what the problem is and how it can be mitigated. Where there are records of nonconformities (or opportunities for improvement[94]) from a previous audit, these should be checked to confirm that corrective actions have been correctly implemented.

15.5.3 The audit programme

As identifying room for improvement is a key audit outcome, with an overall view of continually improving your measures and processes over time, there is little point in conducting an audit as a one-off activity. Establishing a programme of regular audits allows you to identify trends and measure progress over a longer period. Increasing the frequency of your audits will also give you a better chance of becoming aware of nonconformities in a timely manner, before problems can manifest themselves in ways that are externally visible and are usually more costly to fix.

Assuming you aim for annual audits, you do not need to conduct the whole audit once a year in one sitting. It may prove more convenient to break the audit up, for instance, on a departmental basis. This approach can also allow corrective actions to be checked more quickly. As long as you have conducted a full audit within the space of one year, this is a perfectly valid approach.

Your audit programme should ideally schedule audits at a frequency that minimises risk – all key requirements should be covered, but high-risk, frequently used and/or frequently changing processes should be audited more often to minimise the risk of having problems go under the radar for long periods, with potentially serious consequences. By the

---

[94] An opportunity for improvement indicates that a system is in place that meets requirements, but it is implemented in a manner that might allow a problem to manifest further down the line.

same logic, high-level policies and processes infrequently used are less likely to undergo significant changes in a short (or even medium) period of time, so you can afford to audit those less frequently. Where any process sees significant change, however, it should be covered in the next audit to ensure that the changes are effective.

It is also wise to alternate scheduled audits with intermittent unscheduled audits, where auditees are not given a chance to update their documentation days before – and specifically for the sake of – the audit. This will give the best insight into the true day-to-day running of the various business departments, with the best chance of identifying – and fixing – nonconformities.

15.5.4 Reporting to management

Senior management should review and assess the audit reports (or a synopsis of them), with a particular view on major findings that could have significant financial or strategic impact, since they can be a valuable source of independent information on how the organisation is doing, without the risk of bias from operational managers' reports. It can also inform them that additional resources for a particular part of the business may be necessary to resolve the root cause of persistent issues.

Precisely for that independent, unbiased information, it is vital that the auditor reports to senior rather than operational management. Since the latter has a vested interest in the processes being audited, there is a higher chance for conflicts of interest to arise. However, particularly in smaller companies, the line between senior and operational management is often blurred, making it harder to deliver bad news since management line conflicts are more likely. For such situations, outsourcing may be the better solution.

15.6 External certification/validation

> If there is a business need to provide evidence of the strength of your security, such as meeting contractual requirements or providing assurances to stakeholders, you should consider the value of seeking external certification.
>
> **Key output:** Decide whether to pursue external certification based on your security needs and objectives.

Naturally, it is completely possible to have excellent security measures in place without seeking some form of external validation. Organisations might choose to do this to save money, for example, or because they do not see the benefit of being restricted by a given framework. 15.6.1 and 15.6.2 below discuss each of these concerns; however, whether certification is the right avenue to pursue is a decision each organisation needs to make individually based on its security objectives.

If you do decide that you want to make use of widely recognised frameworks, several of them are discussed in more detail in part 5 of this book.

15.6.1 Cost concerns

For organisations concerned about an 'unnecessary' cost, it is worth taking a wider view, and considering the opportunities that certification could bring. Many UK government contracts require Cyber Essentials certification (see 27.1), for example, and it is becoming increasingly common for supplier contracts to require ISO 27001 certification (see 28.2). The idea of such schemes is that an organisation is not just secure, but that they have also proven it to an external, independent party.

In the long term, the fact that you can credibly demonstrate that you take security seriously can prove a decisive factor in winning new business. It proves that you are not just another organisation paying lip service to security – which can be as extreme as declaring something concrete, such as claiming to provide end-to-end encryption – only for that claim to be discredited at a later stage. Zoom Video Communications is an example of this: as a growing number of high-risk vulnerabilities were made public, disproving the company's claims to take security seriously, Zoom has been shunned or outright banned by a growing list of high-profile bodies, including the US Department of Defense and Standard Chartered.[95]

Additionally, for your own peace of mind, the fact that you are able to pass an external audit can help validate your security efforts, alongside other activities discussed in this 'govern and assure' chapter. In effect, a widely recognised framework can give you a baseline to compare your own measures against.

---

[95] Anshuman Daga and Imani Moise, "Exclusive: Stay off Zoom and Google Hangouts, Standard Chartered chief tells staff", *Reuters*, April 2020, *https://www.reuters.com/article/us-health-coronavirus-zoom-exclusive/exclusive-stay-off-zoom-google-hangouts-standard-chartered-chief-tells-staff-idUSKCN21W2PX*.

15.6.2 Flexibility concerns

Some organisations may want to avoid being tied to a particular framework because they do not want to implement controls that they do not need, for example, or do not want to risk losing sight of the primary goal: security measures that enhance business performance, rather than compliance with some framework without developing a true security culture.

Such concerns are valid, and demonstrate an understanding of the potential pitfalls of certification schemes – being so focused on achieving compliance that the journey becomes a box-ticking exercise rather than the development of a security programme that is tailored to your organisation's needs and requirements. However, being aware of that risk at an early stage makes it easier to avoid tunnel vision.

Furthermore, through a combination of the range of schemes available and their tendency to be flexible, that risk is smaller than you may think – after all, many require some form of risk management, with the idea that you address just those risks specific to your organisation in order to achieve compliance. On top of that, many standards are only prescriptive at a high level, leaving room for interpretation, and enabling organisations to implement them as appropriate to their needs and circumstances.

CHAPTER 16: MATURITY LEVELS

The CRF has a further layer beyond the roster of control activities: maturity. As you are probably aware, maturity describes how well developed and integrated an activity (or framework) is. In the context of security, this is a valuable way of understanding both how well you are protecting your organisation and how much further you may need to go in order to meet your organisation's requirements for cyber security and resilience.

The CRF maturity levels, which can be used to measure individual processes as well as the overall framework, are:

1. **Non-existent:**
   The framework/process does not exist, or is not consistent or reliable.
2. **In progress:**
   The organisation is implementing the framework/process or has deployed it across part of the scope.
3. **Established process:**
   The framework/process is in place and applied consistently, and may be improved through automation or software support for consistency, repeatability and robustness.
4. **Established and endorsed by top management:**
   The framework/process is established as above and is overseen by an engaged top management team.

It is important to understand that a higher level of maturity is not automatically 'better'. The level of maturity to aim for entirely depends on your needs and circumstances: if you are not vulnerable to environmental threats, for example, a 'non-existent' level of environmental security would be the most appropriate level of maturity.

Generally speaking, if you need only a basic level of cyber security, the two lower levels of maturity should suffice for a number of your processes and give you the best return on investment – the latter being not only financially favourable, but crucial to securing continued support and resources for your cyber security programme.

Having consistently defined maturity levels will also make it easier to compare your current against your ideal target state (in step 4 of our eight-step approach), giving you a clear overview of where your biggest 'gaps' are. In turn, that information will inform your project plan.

Where there is a big gap between your current and ideal target state, you may want to consider taking an iterative approach towards maturity (a continual improvement model can help with this; see 15.2).

16.1 Determining the level of maturity to aim for

When determining the level of maturity you need for a given CRF process, you should first assess your requirements for it. If, for instance, a contract sets a specific level of consistency in the use of encryption, this will dictate the maturity that you need to achieve.

Equally, your organisation's requirements for cyber security (which you will establish in step 2 of our eight-step approach; see chapter 19) will help determine the necessary maturity for the programme as a whole.

Crucially, your requirements – and the security and project objectives derived from them – form the basis of the maturity levels you set in your ideal target state.

Part 4: Eight steps to implementing cyber security

CHAPTER 17: INTRODUCING THE IT GOVERNANCE EIGHT-STEP APPROACH

This part of the book explains how you can use the CRF to guide your cyber security project, in an eight-step approach that has been put together based on best practice and our tried-and-tested methodology for implementing information security management systems (ISMS).

However, you may have a different preferred method for implementing projects such as this one, or you may want to make slight adjustments to our eight-step approach. For instance, if you just want to be cyber secure, and are not pressured by a specific legal or contractual requirement, it may be better to first conduct a risk assessment (step 6, chapter 23) before you define your target state (step 4, chapter 21).

It is also worth reiterating that the CRF primarily consists of a comprehensive set of controls, which we do not expect you to implement in full, but map against your specific requirements. The CRF is designed for flexible implementation, while helping you identify all the different processes you *may* want to implement, and how to go about it if you choose to do so (as described for individual processes in part 3 of this book).

CHAPTER 18: STEP 1 – START THE PROJECT

It may be something of a cliché but, for cyber security implementation projects, it is certainly true to say that 'well begun is half done'. The person charged with leading the project has to reduce something that looks potentially complex, difficult and expensive in terms of time and resources, to something that everyone believes can be achieved in the time frame allocated and with the resources allowed. And then you have to make sure that it is actually delivered!

What this means in practice is that the project leader has to set up the project in such a way that it is adequately resourced, that there is enough time (including for everything that may go wrong), and that everyone understands the risks in the project and accepts the measures that are being implemented to minimise those risks.

Almost everyone dislikes change. Very few people relish dealing with the unknown. Most will see a cyber security project with any rigour as something that brings both change and the unknown into their working life, and not everyone will welcome it. That is normal – they will get on board in the end, particularly if they see that top management supports the project and start seeing results, which will ultimately strengthen your security culture (also see 12.11.5).

You may also have to overcome other barriers, such as regulatory restrictions, conflicting requirements, and budget or resource limitations. Again, such barriers are normal, but it is important to identify them early on in the project so you can anticipate them and work towards a solution quickly, giving the project the best chance of success. Equally, it is worth identifying project 'enablers' early on, with board support one of the most critical, so you can use them to your advantage from the start.

The project leader, in the first phase of the project, is the person to whom everyone else in the organisation turns for insight, guidance and support. They have to be the person who provides enthusiasm, certainty and an understanding of what is involved. They do not necessarily have extensive technical knowledge, but should have a good understanding of the organisation's requirements and the principles of cyber security best practice.

Equally, that person is likely to have to learn on the job – ultimately, it is not realistic to expect to have all the answers at the outset. Essentially, as long as they have a clear understanding of the strategic issues and practical knowledge of where to turn for advice and guidance, they can be effective – even if they are only a day or two ahead of everyone else in the detailed knowledge required for the project.

18.1 Project mandate

The project mandate is the first document you should develop. It begins as a statement of what you wish to achieve that can be approved by the board or leadership team, and will grow over time into a clearer statement of the project's goals.

From the very start of the project, it is important that you document everything. Establishing a project mandate at this stage, even if you cannot provide much detail in every section yet, will help ensure you keep a record of all decisions, commitments, etc. already made, and provide a clear reference point. One particularly important point to capture early on in your project mandate is the initial evidence of board-level commitment (also see 15.3) – which is essential to the success of the project, even more so than choosing the right project leader from the start – in a usable format.

As you progress to the later stages of the project, you can continue to refer to and expand this early document. Ultimately, a project mandate should capture the key elements of any complex project, cyber security included, ensuring there is a single, original point of reference that sets out the three keys to project success: deliverables, timeline and budget.

When complex projects fail, it is because one or more of these three project variables are poorly identified and/or managed. 'Scope creep' is one of the most common roots of project failure. Project mandates, therefore, seek to clearly identify project scope and to pin down the three variables in order to support an effective project governance process. (In our eight-step approach, scope is finalised in step 3 in chapter 20.)

Your project mandate should address these four points:

1. **Deliverables**: identify why cyber security is important for your organisation and what you want to get out of your implementation project. For now, it is sufficient to pin down why you are embarking on this project in the first place – in step 2 (chapter 19) you will identify more specifically what your requirements and objectives are, and document them.

2. **Timeline**: create an outline project plan and target completion date.
3. **Budget**: identify the resources, both internal and external, that you are going to need for the project.
4. **Authorisation to proceed**: the mandate should contain management endorsement of the project and authorisation to proceed, to achieve the identified objectives using the budgeted resources.

18.2 Project team

As part of putting together your pre-project documents, you should have determined who the project leader will be. At this point, you would ideally start creating a RACI matrix for the project. This identifies who should be **R**esponsible, **A**ccountable, **C**onsulted and **I**nformed regarding key project decisions and each of the cyber security management processes as they are drawn up.

The project team should be made up of roles that have responsibility for representing the interests of every key part of the organisation; this does not mean that every part of the organisation must be directly represented, as that would almost certainly create a huge and unwieldy team, but that each person on the team should be aware of whose interests they need to look out for.

Ideally, the people invited to represent different organisational functions should be among the most senior, experienced and widely respected individuals within them. As mentioned earlier, effective cyber security will require a security culture (see 12.11.5). When just starting with cyber security, this almost certainly requires a cultural change, albeit to varying degrees depending on the organisation. It is critical that those most able to represent and articulate the needs and concerns of the key parts of the organisation are included in the working party. Without their involvement, there is unlikely to be the buy-in necessary for cyber security measures to be effectively developed and implemented.

Perhaps obviously, the team should also include at least one experienced project manager, who will be responsible for tracking and reporting progress against the planned objectives.

Crucially, balance is important. An effective cyber security programme depends on everyone in the organisation understanding and applying its controls and, if the project team is made up of a preponderance of non-technical people, it is more likely to produce something that everyone in the organisation can understand.

Besides the representation of internal stakeholders on the project team, remember that there are also external stakeholders who have a vested interest in your organisation's cyber security, such as customers, partners, suppliers, regulators, etc., who may influence your requirements and/or processes. Project team members need to be able to identify the needs of those stakeholders. The stakeholders themselves should be identified as you start the project, with a view to making the list more specific as the implementation project progresses, and relevant external parties become more apparent.

The project team should report directly to senior management, or (preferably) the CEO, and should have the appropriate delegated authority to implement the project plan.

18.3 Project leadership

Unless the CEO is personally leading the project, the person in charge of the project should ask for the following active support:

- That the CEO makes a point of understanding the business benefits of pursuing a cyber security strategy, and the return on investment this project will achieve for the organisation.
- That the CEO leads a presentation (for the project leader to prepare) on the cyber security strategy to the board, includes the primary project objective(s) in the organisation's business goals for the year, secures board support for the objective(s) expressed in the project mandate and arranges for ongoing board monitoring of project progress throughout its life (which will ensure the project achieves and maintains the sort of political profile that will improve its chances of success).
- That the CEO personally leads presentations (for the project leader to prepare) on the project to the senior management of the organisation as well as to all staff via organisational forums used for staff communication, and clearly sets out – for everyone in the organisation, including senior management – the prioritisation for this project and the project leader's authority to seek the input and involvement of all whose contribution will be essential to the project's success.
- That the CEO sets a personal example of applying all the work practices and following all the procedures that will become part of the new cyber security programme,

and welcomes challenges from staff if they think the CEO is not following a procedure.

CHAPTER 19: STEP 2 – DETERMINE REQUIREMENTS AND OBJECTIVES

There may have been a specific requirement that prompted your organisation to embark on a cyber security project, and for you to read this book. Now that you are embarking on a full cyber security programme, however, it is important to move beyond the catalyst and look at the bigger picture.

What other legal and/or contractual requirements must you meet? Are there sector-specific requirements you need to consider? What are your competitors and partners doing? What do customers expect? What key products and services must be available to ensure you can do business? For a truly effective and sustainable programme, your business requirements must be considered alongside your legal, contractual and sector-specific requirements. Only then can your cyber security programme be an active means of generating revenue, and not just a compliance expense.

19.1 Project vs cyber security objectives

Once you have established the full range of requirements you must meet – whether imposed externally or to meet business goals – you can use them as the basis for defining and documenting your objectives. These should draw a distinction between project and cyber security objectives.

Project objectives refer to things such as achieving compliance with regulatory or contractual requirements within a certain time frame. They may also refer to compliance with a particular code, standard or framework, such as Cyber Essentials or ISO 27001. In other words, project objectives link specifically to the business benefits of implementing cyber security. Such objectives are typically high-level, and are relatively easy to track. Accountability for their achievement lies with the top of the organisation.

Cyber security objectives may be, but are not necessarily, related to the project objectives. Cyber (and information) security objectives will definitely be linked to the preservation of the CIA of information and IT assets, and in relation to the organisation's risk tolerance. Progress towards achieving your security objectives must be measurable, which means the objectives themselves need to be specific, measurable, achievable, realistic and time-bound.

Typical objectives might, for instance, be to reduce the number of security incidents from 14 to two per year, or to increase network availability from 97% and 20×7×360 to 99.9% and 24×7×365. Such objectives will be broken down into lower-level objectives, with accountability for their achievement allocated to appropriate departments and levels within the organisation.

CHAPTER 20: STEP 3 – DETERMINE THE SCOPE

Project scoping is fundamental. You need to know the boundaries of what you are planning to implement, which you can derive from the objectives you established in step 2 (chapter 19).

Scope determination is harder for larger, more complex organisations than it is for smaller ones. However, scoping is essential whatever your size: you have to decide which information and IT assets you are going to protect and which ones you are not, before you can decide on appropriate protection. To avoid trying to draw the boundaries too narrowly, make sure that you can justify any exclusions. It is also important to double-check that your scope covers all your requirements and objectives determined in step 2.

For a small- or medium-sized business, the decision should be quick: the whole organisation. This is because there will probably be hard-wired connections between all the information systems and day-to-day working relationships within the business that make it either extremely difficult or impractical to try to segregate one part of the business from another.

The notion of segregation is at the heart of effective scoping: ultimately, you are going to try to create an impregnable barrier between the part of your business that is within the scope of your project and everything else. You have to be categorical about what is inside your information fortress and what is outside – *no* information systems, devices or business units should be both inside *and* outside, because that would be your weak point in the wall.

With remote working becoming increasingly common, your defensive barrier has to operate at the individual device level and is highly dependent on user compliance with business procedures. In other words, your scoping decision needs to include all the information devices that people use in their jobs – be it laptops, smartphones or tablets – as well as the more obvious central office systems such as accounting, payment processing, production, sales and order management, email, office automation, etc. Be sure to also take relevant Cloud-based components into account.

CHAPTER 21: STEP 4 – DEFINE CURRENT AND IDEAL TARGET STATES

Most organisations already have some cyber security measures in place – these may not be sufficient or as effective as they should be, but the point is that you are almost certainly not starting from scratch. It is therefore important to understand how far your current practices are from where you want to be.

Before you can do that, you have to define both your current and ideal target states in a way that they can easily be compared against one another. The CRF can make this task easier.

Using the CRF

The most pertinent parts of the CRF for this process are the comprehensive selection of processes (discussed in detail in part 3 of this book) and the different levels of maturity (see chapter 16). The Framework recognises that few organisations need every single process within it, and the processes that *are* required may not need to be very mature for your purposes.

This level of detail and flexibility means that the Framework is an effective tool for helping you define your current and target states. The clearly defined maturity levels, meanwhile, make for straightforward and consistent comparisons between your two states.

Appendix 2 offers a template project plan that you can use to indicate which controls you already have in place, and to what level of maturity, in the 'Current state' column. In the final row you should indicate your overall current level of maturity.

In the final row of the 'Ideal target state' column you can also indicate the overall level of maturity that you intend to achieve – you should be able to derive this from the objectives you defined in step 2 (chapter 19). Where your objectives are specific enough (such as compliance with a specifically defined set of requirements, such as the PCI DSS), you can also start filling in target maturity levels for individual controls.

If you are simply looking to be cyber secure, without necessarily being driven by a specific legal or contractual requirement, it may be better for you to first conduct a risk assessment (step 6) and select your controls (step 7, chapter 24) based on that, which you can then use to inform your project plan.

Gap analysis

After you have established both your current and ideal target states at the level of individual processes (also see appendix 2), you should conduct what we call a 'gap analysis'. This is a quick, high-level audit or comparison of your current against your target practices, identifying where there is a shortfall.

On the basis of the gap analysis, you then establish:

- Who should be the owner of each process, making sure that no single person is unduly burdened;
- The actions you need to take to close the gaps, where they exist;
- When those actions should be complete; and

- What resources and capabilities you have internally, or need to bring in from outside the organisation, to be able to take those actions within the intended time frame.

At this stage, it is perfectly acceptable for your outline project plan to be quite high-level, primarily making key objectives and timelines clear. As the details of your project become clearer, so will your project plan. You will, however, still want to stay within the original timelines and avoid disruptions to the project that could have an impact on the timeline you have committed to achieving.

CHAPTER 22: STEP 5 – ESTABLISH A CONTINUAL IMPROVEMENT MODEL

Whatever continual improvement method or model you use, and wherever your inputs come from, it is critical that it is cyclical to ensure you keep your improvements both regular and manageable. Some example methods are discussed in more depth in 15.2.3 and 15.2.4.

Continual improvement is not just something you do at the end of a project, however. Particularly for a more complex project, as cyber security may well be, it can be a useful way of taking an incremental, step-by-step approach to implementation, with brief reviews between each step to make sure that you are heading in the right direction and that your target state is still relevant.[96]

To enable that incremental, manageable approach for the remainder of the implementation project, you need to determine your continual improvement methodology before you conduct a risk assessment and start implementing controls. Use the output of your gap analysis from step 4 (see chapter 21) as a starting point, and think about how you might break the work up into steps or phases. After you conduct a risk assessment and choose controls, you can

[96] It is important to commit to what you set out to achieve, of course, but both business environments and the cyber threat landscape are prone to rapid change, so it is important to maintain a degree of flexibility, particularly if you expect the project to span several months or even years.

further detail your work plan, prioritising the most important and high-risk areas.

Make sure to regularly review your work and incorporate improvement initiatives, with progress documented in your continual improvement log. Interim results should be presented to management so they can see that progress is being made, and to continue securing their support.

CHAPTER 23: STEP 6 – CONDUCT A RISK ASSESSMENT

Risk assessment has already been discussed in detail in 12.12, so will not be discussed in much more depth here. However, it is worth looking at a condensed version of security guru Bruce Schneier's five steps (or questions) that are intended as a mechanism for judging whether a certain security trade-off is worth making.[97] The five questions are:

1. What assets are you trying to protect?
2. What are the risks to those assets?
3. How well does the security solution mitigate the risk?
4. What other risks does the security solution cause?
5. What trade-offs does the security solution require?

It is a straightforward approach that covers all the key points of making sensible security decisions. The first question overlaps with step 3 of this book's eight-step approach (see chapter 20), determining the scope of implementation. The remaining questions effectively constitute a risk assessment.

Ultimately, you need to limit yourself to the scope of your project, decide what risks are applicable, as well as what controls best mitigate them, considering their effectiveness and drawbacks, and whether that trade-off is worth it. In

---

[97] Bruce Schneier, *Beyond Fear: Thinking Sensibly About Security in an Uncertain World*, Copernicus Books, 2003, pp. 14–15. Although this book may date back to 2003, many of its principles, including these five steps, are still applicable today.

addition, remember to consider what your greatest risks are, and which you need to prioritise.

CHAPTER 24: STEP 7 – SELECT AND IMPLEMENT CONTROLS

Your intended risk treatments are likely to fall within the CRF processes, telling you which ones you need and to what level of maturity you should aim to implement each, and by extension enabling you to refine your project plan (see appendix 2).

Where there is a large gap between your current and target states, it is sensible to take an iterative approach, making use of the continual improvement model you established in step 5 (chapter 22) and prioritising the controls that address the biggest risks. It is important, however, that each iteration maintains a balance between the three security pillars – people, processes and technology (see 5.2).

Remember that the full set of controls you implement may be larger than the set of controls you identify in your risk assessment. These extra controls will be defined by the legal, contractual and sector-specific requirements you have identified. It is entirely possible that these requirements do not address a risk you actually face, or that the risk is relatively low, but that they are simply mandated by a customer, a regulator, the government or some other stakeholder.

CHAPTER 25: STEP 8 – MEASURE AND REVIEW PERFORMANCE

Your cyber security programme will only be useful – and sustainable – if you can show that your cyber security and project objectives are being met. For this, measurement of the logs and outputs of the controls implemented in step 7 (see chapter 24) is essential. These measurements should be designed so that you can compare the information you gain now to measurements you take in the future. (Measurement was briefly covered in 15.1.2.)

For the best results and a consistent approach from the start, you should plan the measurement as you plan the implementation of the control. It could be a good idea to run short tests to prove that the measurement provides reproducible results before putting it into action. It is also important that you measure at regular, planned intervals – ideally at least annually – and when significant changes occur.

Of course, it can prove very expensive to measure absolutely every control, not to mention that measuring everything is not necessary to get meaningful results and see a clear return on investment, so selectiveness is important. When identifying which controls to measure, prioritise those that are:

- Intended to mitigate the highest risks;
- Most likely to fail;
- The most expensive to implement, maintain or repair; and
- The most complex.

Be aware that, when selecting controls and determining how they will be measured, the act of measurement itself affects the behaviour of the people being measured. For example, measuring how long it takes to perform a certain task may result in employees prioritising the *speed* at which that task is performed over the *quality* of the task, which can have a negative impact on the process despite the good intention. It is important to ensure that the measurements you select do not drive behaviour that is detrimental to the process.

25.1 Continual improvement

Naturally, your measurement activities may indicate that some controls are not working as well as intended. Identified areas for improvement can be used as inputs for your cyclical continual improvement efforts. After implementing the improvement, the performance of the control in question should be measured again, with further changes made if necessary.

The measurements themselves should also be subject to continual improvement. This does not mean that you need to measure your measurements, but you should be able to demonstrate, at some point, that your measurement system is improving. To do this, you can take either a quantitative or a qualitative approach.

A quantitative approach might involve reviewing trends in measurement results to determine if the measurements being used are appropriate, and retiring or adding measurements as necessary. This approach can be particularly useful while your cyber security programme is still relatively new, as it allows you to ensure that the measurements you are taking are appropriate, provide useful information and do not drive detrimental behaviour.

A qualitative approach, meanwhile, could involve surveying the owners of the processes being measured. Experienced process owners are likely to be aware of any flaws in the measurement system as it relates to their process, and their input can be an invaluable tool for improvement. This method is useful in later phases of your programme, where changes (new hardware, software, etc.) may have affected the measurement being performed.

25.2 Management review

Senior management must be able to see that the overall programme is achieving its intended results, and meeting regulatory, contractual and business requirements. A management review supports this by assessing condensed, high-level information from measurement, relevant logs, internal audit reports (where applicable; see 15.5) and any other continual improvement activity, so that management can plan and review the strategic direction of the programme and ensure its ongoing effectiveness. They should also check the progress of any corrections identified in the last management review.

Such reviews should take place on a regular basis, and might be relatively frequent – perhaps quarterly – while the programme is still being developed and gaining steam. Once the programme is well embedded, they might only be conducted annually. There is an element of management's confidence in the programme that will determine the exact frequency.

Management are in the best position to identify where corrective action is necessary for any noted deficiencies, and to highlight requirements that may have changed (such as a new law that has come into force, or to account for a new market). Any new requirements can be checked against current review data to determine what the organisation might need to do. This is then directed to your continual improvement process to support planning changes to your cyber security controls and inform their ongoing development.

To give senior management the best oversight of the programme, they need to receive independent, unbiased information. As such, it is important that your measurement system and any other inputs to the management review process give consistent and repeatable results. Furthermore, the results should be presented in a balanced, neutral way to ensure they are not skewed (or perceived to be) to suit an agenda.

Management reviews can be time-consuming, so it is important to plan ahead to ensure sufficient management availability. In very large or complex organisations with lots of data to cover, it may be beneficial to conduct the review over the course of several sessions rather than attempt to cover everything in a single session. Regardless of how the management review is conducted, ensure you keep clear records (for example, meeting minutes) to inform future reviews.

Part 5: Reference frameworks

CHAPTER 26: WHY YOU SHOULD CONSIDER REFERENCE FRAMEWORKS

It is perfectly possible to develop a robust cyber security system without using internationally recognised standards or frameworks. Indeed, if you purely viewed part 3 of this book as a reference, rather than the building blocks of our resilience framework, and just implemented the most basic and relevant controls discussed, you are already off to a great start. As your cyber security posture evolves, however, you may find that standards or frameworks can benefit your organisation in several ways.[98]

Standards and frameworks offer a tried, tested and comprehensive approach to cyber security developed by experts in the field. By adopting such an approach, you can take some of the guesswork out of developing or improving your own system, enhancing your defences in line with recognised industry best practice and accounting for aspects of cyber security that you might not otherwise have considered.

Additionally, many standards are significantly less prescriptive now than they used to be. As a result, when you implement them, you should only be spending money on the controls you truly need.

---

[98] If you are interested in how the CRF and the frameworks discussed in this part of the book overlap, check the end of chapters 27-30, where there are tables that provide an overview of that alignment.

26.1 Standard types

There are generally two types of standard. Some are declaratory and rely on the organisation itself to demonstrate conformity, while others allow for independent verification of conformity by an external party, but both types generally take a comprehensive approach that accounts for the wider organisation in relevant areas.

Frameworks are lists of controls and accompanying guidance, and are often more focused than standards. Frameworks are usually developed by third-sector and commercial organisations, which means that they tend to be more up to date than standards (the update process for an international standard usually takes around five years, if not longer, and requires extensive stakeholder negotiation, while third-sector and commercial organisations tend to be less restricted in this regard), but they rarely allow for independent verification.

There are standards and frameworks suitable for organisations of all sizes and all levels of cyber security experience. Besides the level of maturity you require, it is also important to consider what standards or frameworks are recognised in the regions in which you operate – for instance, conforming to the NIST Cybersecurity Framework (CSF) (see 28.1) more likely earns you plaudits in the US than outside of it.

In this final part of the book, we discuss a number of best-practice standards and frameworks, each with their own strengths and drawbacks, which should give you an idea of the range available. However, the ones covered here are only the tip of the iceberg, and it is best – assuming you want to make use of a standard or a framework – if you conduct your own research into what other suitable options are available to your industry and operating region(s).

How far you go in applying a standard or framework is up to you. Some organisations use standards that allow for certification but forego the certification process while still applying the advice, guidance and requirements – this gives most of the benefits of the standard without the need to pay for the certification process, or the longer-term cost of audits and other verification activities.

26.2 Certification benefits

Certification (discussed in more detail in 15.6) should not be dismissed lightly. Independently verified cyber security is the one thing that will assure current and prospective clients that you take an industry-recognised, best-practice approach to cyber security. It can also save money by allowing you to demonstrate effective cyber security in a format recognised by your clients and partners, reducing the need for them to verify it through additional audits that drain time and resources on both sides.

On top of that, if you want cyber insurance, certification could also be a prerequisite or help lower your premiums. Finally, even if certification itself is not an explicit requirement, it can still be a solid way of demonstrating that your organisation has appropriate technical and organisational security measures in place – a common contractual and legal requirement.

In many cases, adoption of standards and frameworks is driven by business need – a potential client or investor expects a certain level of cyber security and insists that you adopt a standard or framework to prove that you can achieve and maintain it as a condition of doing business. Although you can implement cyber security standards at a client's request, doing so often results in rushed development and ineffective systems. It is better to identify and adopt the most suitable standard or framework before it becomes a topic of negotiation, so you can implement it at your own pace without external pressure.

CHAPTER 27: CORE

One way to approach standards and frameworks, especially if you are not sure whether they are right for your organisation, is to start small and work your way up. The more basic frameworks can also be a good way of generally getting started with cyber security, as they tend to be affordable and relatively straightforward to implement.

27.1 Cyber Essentials

Cyber Essentials is a UK government scheme supported by the NCSC, and is intended to help organisations of any size demonstrate their commitment to cyber security, while keeping the approach simple and the costs low.

The scheme focuses on five key cyber security controls, which are basic yet protect organisations from around 80% of common cyber attacks, and has two tiers of achievement:

1. Cyber Essentials; and
2. Cyber Essentials Plus.

The five basic security controls that both tiers require are:

1. Firewalls;
2. Secure configuration;
3. Access control;
4. Malware protection; and
5. Patch management.

As basic as these controls and as straightforward as the certification process might be, it is still vital that you determine your scope (as discussed in chapter 20) before your project can truly get underway. Cyber Essentials certification can apply to all or a subset of your enterprise IT, which must meet certain conditions, and may include hardware and software.

Once you have defined the scope, you can proceed to the self-assessment questionnaire (or 'SAQ') and an external vulnerability scan that both Cyber Essentials tiers require. The 'Plus' tier also requires an on-site assessment and an additional internal vulnerability scan, providing additional assurance both for you and your clients. Certification to either tier also provides numerous other benefits, including the ability to tender for business where certification to the scheme is a prerequisite and reduces insurance premiums. In fact, all UK organisations with a turnover of less than £20 million (about $25 million) that achieve Cyber Essentials certification covering the whole organisation receive cyber insurance with a total liability limit of £25,000 (about $32,000).[99]

It may seem surprising that these basic controls can already bring such vast benefits, but there has been more than one breach where it turned out that at least one of these controls was not in place. For instance, consider a breach suffered by international airline Cathay Pacific, for which it was fined the maximum fine under the UK's Data Protection Act (DPA) 1998 (now superseded by the EU GDPR and UK

[99] For more information on how to achieve Cyber Essentials/Cyber Essentials Plus certification, see: https://www.itgovernance.co.uk/cyber-essentials-scheme.

DPA 2018).[100] It failed no fewer than three Cyber Essentials controls: the "catalogue of errors" uncovered by the UK data protection watchdog included a lack of access controls (backup files were not password-protected), inadequate malware protection and poor patch management (there were unpatched Internet-facing servers and operating systems no longer supported by the developer).

It is certainly worth remembering that failing to put in place the most basic cyber security measures – which are typically also the easiest and cheapest to implement – likely leads to the biggest fines if you are subject to a regulatory investigation or audit.

27.2 CRF alignment

The following table shows how the CRF and Cyber Essentials align:

[100] ICO, "International airline fined £500,000 for failing to secure its customers' personal data", March 2020, *https://ico.org.uk/about-the-ico/news-and-events/news-and-blogs/2020/03/international-airline-fined-500-000-for-failing-to-secure-its-customers-personal-data*.

Table 7: How Cyber Essentials and the CRF Align

	Core	
	Cyber Essentials	*CRF*
Manage and protect		
Asset management		
Information security policies		
Physical and environmental security		
Identity and access control	✓	12.4
Malware protection	✓	12.5
Configuration and patch management	✓	12.6
Encryption		
System security	✓	12.8
Network and communications security	✓	12.9
Security competence and training		
Staff awareness training		
Comprehensive risk management programme		

Supply chain risk management		
Identify and detect		
Threat and vulnerability intelligence		
Security monitoring		
Respond and recover		
Incident response management		
ICT continuity management		
Business continuity management		
Govern and assure		
Formal information security management programme		
Continual improvement process		
Board-level commitment and involvement		
Governance structure and processes		
Internal audit		
External certification/ validation	✓	15.6

CHAPTER 28: BASELINE

If Cyber Essentials does not go far enough, or if you are looking for something recognised outside the UK, then your next stop will almost certainly be the NIST CSF (see 28.1) or ISO 27001 (see 28.2). Both form a good baseline for starting to develop a solid cyber security framework.

28.1 NIST CSF

The NIST CSF offers a straightforward yet flexible framework. The Framework can help organisations establish a new cyber security programme or improve existing practices, and can be implemented alongside other frameworks such as ISO 27001 (see 28.2). Combining a standard you can certify against with the NIST CSF can be a good idea, as the latter lacks a certification pathway but is intended to be highly tailorable.

There are three main components in the NIST CSF: the 'core', the 'profiles' and the 'implementation tiers'.

The core comprises an organisation's cyber security activities and controls, and is subdivided into four levels of detail. At the highest level there are five 'functions' that outline how to organise your cyber security activities:

1. **Identify** the risks.
2. **Protect** yourself against these risks by implementing appropriate measures.
3. **Detect** any anomalies to identify possible breaches.
4. **Respond** to any breaches identified.
5. **Recover** from those breaches.

Each function is then divided into 'categories', which describe general cyber security activities and their intended outcomes. In turn, categories are divided into 'subcategories', which describe the specific results of the activities required to fulfil each category. Finally, each subcategory is aligned to 'informative references' – sources of best practices, drawn from a range of publications, including some of the standards covered in this part of the book.

The NIST CSF core's fairly broad approach to security, particularly the five functions, is one that aligns to internationally accepted best practices, and indeed the IT Governance CRF. The idea is that you do not just aim to minimise the likelihood and impact of cyber incidents, but also prepare for an effective response and recovery on the assumption that a breach can happen in spite of your best efforts.

The next main component of the NIST CSF is the 'profiles', which are a means of identifying what actions the organisation needs to take to become secure. The 'current profile' describes how cyber security is currently handled, and the 'target profile' describes the organisation's security aspirations. Much like step 4 in our eight-step approach to implementing cyber security, comparing the two profiles gives you the starting point for your action plan.

The third and final main NIST CSF component is the four 'implementation tiers' ('partial', 'risk-informed', 'repeatable' and 'adaptive'), which describe the rigour of the organisation's risk management and other cyber security measures. Like our levels of maturity (see Chapter 16), a higher tier is not automatically better – they simply describe the degree of sophistication of the organisation's processes.

28.2 ISO 27001

International standard ISO/IEC 27001 describes the specification for a best-practice ISMS – a systematic approach to managing information security risk across the whole organisation.

ISO 27001 describes 114 reference information security controls (in 14 categories) that you can apply to improve your information security. The 14 categories are:

1. A.5 Information security policies
2. A.6 Organization of information security
3. A.7 Human resource security
4. A.8 Asset management
5. A.9 Access control
6. A.10 Cryptography
7. A.11 Physical and environmental security
8. A.12 Operations security
9. A.13 Communications security
10. A.14 System acquisition, development and maintenance
11. A.15 Supplier relationships
12. A.16 Information security incident management
13. A.17 Information security aspects of business continuity management
14. A.18 Compliance

The idea is that you only apply the controls relevant to you, as determined by a risk assessment that meets certain requirements also set out in this standard.

Organisations can seek independent certification against the requirements of ISO 27001 to prove to clients and partners that they take a recognised best-practice approach to information security. There is, however, a larger ISO/IEC 27000 family of standards, of which ISO/IEC 27002 is the most noteworthy.

Where ISO 27001 prescribes the features of an effective ISMS, ISO 27002 provides the code of conduct – recommended best practices that can be used to enforce the specification, providing guidance for selecting controls and implementing an effective ISMS. Essentially, ISO 27002 is designed to assist with effective ISO 27001 implementation.

There are, however, more standards in the ISO 27000 family that may help. ISO/IEC 27005, for instance, provides guidance for information security risk management in line with ISO 27001, intended to help organisations take a risk-based approach to information security.

Meanwhile, ISO 27017 offers a code of practice for information security controls when providing or using Cloud services (discussed further in 29.2), ISO 27035 offers guidance on information security incident management (see 29.3) and ISO 27036 provides guidelines on securing the supply chain (see 29.4). These standards may be of particular benefit to organisations looking to achieve a more mature level of security.

Because ISO 27001 uses the same base format as other management system standards, it can also be combined with an existing management system (such as an ISO 9001 quality management system or 'QMS') to create an integrated management system. This allows you to streamline common activities such as internal audits, saving money over the long term.

28.3 CRF alignment

The following table shows how our CRF, the NIST CSF and ISO 27001 align:

Table 8: How NIST CSF, ISO 27001 and the CRF Align

	Baseline		CRF
	NIST CSF	*ISO 27001*	
Manage and protect			
Asset management	✓	✓	12.1
Information security policies	✓	✓	12.2
Physical and environmental security	✓	✓	12.3
Identity and access control	✓	✓	12.4
Malware protection	✓	✓	12.5
Configuration and patch management	✓	✓	12.6
Encryption	✓	✓	12.7
System security	✓	✓	12.8

Network and communications security	✓	✓	12.9
Security competence and training	✓	✓	12.10
Staff awareness training	✓	✓	12.11
Comprehensive risk management programme	✓	✓	12.12
Supply chain risk management	✓	✓	12.13
Identify and detect			
Threat and vulnerability intelligence	✓	✓	13.1
Security monitoring	✓	✓	13.2
Respond and recover			
Incident response management	✓	✓	14.1
ICT continuity management	✓	✓	14.2

Business continuity management			
Govern and assure			
Formal information security management programme	✓	✓	15.1
Continual improvement process	✓	✓	15.2
Board-level commitment and involvement	✓	✓	15.3
Governance structure and processes			
Internal audit		✓	15.5
External certification/ validation		✓	15.6

CHAPTER 29: EXTENDED

Your baseline framework can be extended with more specialised standards and frameworks – focusing on areas such as business continuity (see 29.1), incident response (see 29.2), Cloud and supply chain security (see 29.3) and privacy management (see 29.4) – to help you build a more comprehensive cyber resilience stance.

29.1 ISO 22301 – BCM

International standard ISO 22301 provides the specification for an effective business continuity management system (BCMS), and can be an excellent addition to ISO 27001 if you are considering an integrated management system – the ISO 27001 and ISO 22301 combination covers the two most fundamental aspects of cyber resilience: information security and business continuity. Like ISO 27001, ISO 22301 also allows for independently verified certification to provide that extra level of assurance to your clients and partners.

The most important principles of BCM, formal or otherwise, are discussed in 14.3. Here, we provide an overview of ISO 22301's most fundamental principles and activities:

- **Securing management support:**
  Like board support for your overall cyber security project (see 15.3), a successful BCMS implementation requires board and/or senior management support – otherwise, the management system could probably not be sustained, as resources are less likely to be sufficient and staff are less likely to be engaged.

- **BIA:**
  The BIA (discussed in more detail in 14.3.1), alongside the risk assessment, is the most critical process involved in a BCMS. It is used to identify an organisation's critical activities and resources, and how severe the business impact would be if those activities were disrupted or those resources unavailable. This information is then used to determine priorities for recovery following a disruption.
- **Risk assessment:**
  Again, as with cyber security (see 12.12 for a detailed discussion on security risk assessments), you can only make informed decisions about how and when to continue key business functions, and make the necessary preparations, if you understand what scenarios might disrupt them in the first place. Your business continuity risk assessment should also establish how likely these disruptive scenarios are, and how severe their impact might be.
- **One or more business continuity plans:**
  These should be developed on the basis of the BIA and risk assessment, and regularly tested to ensure they work as intended.
- **Continual improvement:**
  Continual improvement (also see 15.2) is a feature common to all ISO management systems. The idea is that all business continuity practices and activities are regularly tested and reviewed, with opportunities for improvement identified and implemented. That way,

your business continuity processes become more and more rigorous over time, which will in turn improve your continuity plans.

29.2 ISO 27017 – Cloud security

ISO 27017, which is part of the ISO 27000 family, is a code of practice for information security controls in the Cloud. Specifically, it takes the guidance from ISO 27002, and makes it more applicable for Cloud users, so they can implement appropriate controls, and Cloud providers, so they can support the implementation of such controls. The reasoning behind having a standard specifically on Cloud security is that the nature of Cloud computing introduces risks not seen in other types of computing.

In addition to elaborations, where necessary, on the controls from ISO 27002, ISO 27017 also introduces seven further controls that address Cloud-specific features:

- CLD.6.3.1 Shared roles and responsibilities within a Cloud computing environment
- CLD.8.1.5 Removal of Cloud service customer assets
- CLD.9.5.1 Segregation in virtual computing environments
- CLD.9.5.2 Virtual machine hardening
- CLD.12.1.5 Administrator's operational security
- CLD.12.4.5 Monitoring of Cloud services
- CLD.13.1.4 Alignment of security management for virtual and physical networks

29.3 ISO 27035 – Information security incident management

ISO 27035, another member of the ISO 27000 family, offers guidance on information security incident management. This standard comes in two parts: the first outlines the principles of incident management; the second contains guidelines to plan and prepare for incident response. ISO 27035 has five phases for information security incident management:

1. **Plan and prepare:**
   Completing certain preparatory activities to ensure the incident response plan can be effectively activated and executed when it is necessary.
2. **Detection and reporting:**
   Detecting, collecting information relating to and reporting information security events (that may or may not be an actual incident). This can happen automatically, manually or through a combination of both.
3. **Assessment and decision:**
   Assessing the information on detected events and deciding whether each event should be classed as an incident or not.
4. **Responses:**
   Responding to actual incidents in line with the actions decided in the previous phase.
5. **Lessons learnt:**
   After the incident has been resolved, reviewing actions and controls to identify possible improvements. The Standard explicitly says that information security

incident management activities are supposed to be iterative.

Incident management independent of ISO 27035 (or any other standard) is discussed in more detail in 14.1.

29.4 ISO 27036 – Information security in the supply chain

This four-part standard gives guidance on securing the supply chain. Most organisations will find the second and third parts (ISO 27036-2 and ISO 27036-3) most valuable, which respectively cover the requirements for information security for supplier relationships (irrespective of size or sector) and guidelines for securing the ICT supply chain.

ISO 27036-2 has structured its requirements around the following life cycle:

- Supplier relationship planning process.
- Supplier selection process.
- Supplier relationship agreement process.
- Supplier relationship management process.
- Supplier relationship termination process.

ISO 27036-3 recognises that because ICT services can be provided at a physical distance and are often delivered through several levels of subcontracting, users lack visibility into the full ICT supply chain, creating risk to the acquiring organisation that needs to be managed. Structurally, it mirrors the above life cycle, but discusses individual processes at a more granular level (acquisition process, supply process, life cycle model management process, etc.).

29.5 ISO 27701 – Privacy management

Introduced to fill the assurance gap and provide a genuinely international approach to data protection as an extension of information security, ISO 27701 extends the requirements of ISO 27001 to include privacy management and the security of PII. It recognises that information security is a key aspect of effective privacy management, and that the ISMS requirements from ISO 27001 can support adding sector-specific requirements onto the ISMS without the need for a new management system specification.

ISO 27701 defines the extra requirements for an ISMS to cover privacy and PII processing. These are supported by additional controls that relate specifically to data protection and privacy. As a new whole, this creates what the Standard calls a 'privacy information management system (PIMS)'.

As for accredited certification to ISO 27701, the schemes available at the time of writing do not accommodate that option. Organisations can, however, refer to ISO 27701 as a source of controls in a Statement of Applicability (SoA) cited in an accredited certification document for ISO 27001.

29.6 CRF alignment

The following table shows how our CRF, ISO 22301, ISO 27017, ISO 27035, parts 2 and 3 of ISO 27036 and ISO 27701 align:

Table 9: How Notable ISO Standards Align with the CRF

	Extended					CRF
	ISO 22301	*ISO 27017**	*ISO 27035*	*ISO 27036*	*ISO 27701**	
Manage and protect						
Asset management		✓	✓	✓	✓	12.1
Information security policies		✓	✓	✓	✓	12.2
Physical and environmental security				✓	✓	12.3
Identity and access control		✓		✓	✓	12.4
Malware protection				✓		12.5
Configuration and patch management				✓		12.6
Encryption		✓		✓	✓	12.7
System security		✓		✓	✓	12.8
Network and communications security				✓	✓	12.9
Security competence and training			✓	✓		12.10

Staff awareness training		✓		✓	✓	12.11
Comprehensive risk management programme	✓	✓	✓	✓	✓	12.12
Supply chain risk management		✓	✓	✓	✓	12.13
Identify and detect						
Threat and vulnerability intelligence			✓			13.1
Security monitoring		✓	✓			13.2
Respond and recover						
Incident response management	✓	✓	✓	✓	✓	14.1
ICT continuity management			✓	✓		14.2
Business continuity management	✓					14.3
Govern and assure						
Formal information security management programme		✓	✓	✓	✓	15.1

Continual improvement process	✓		✓			15.2
Board-level commitment and involvement	✓		✓	✓	✓	15.3
Governance structure and processes						
Internal audit	✓					15.5
External certification/ validation	✓				✓ **	15.6

* Only includes control expansions or additions (compared to the guidance in ISO 27001 and ISO 27002).

** Only in combination with ISO 27001; see 28.2 and 28.3 for details.

CHAPTER 30: EMBEDDED

At this stage, you should have developed your base framework and extended it as your specific needs demand, drawing on best-practice standards and frameworks where appropriate. Now, you should think about how you can align your cyber resilience objectives and activities with your wider business objectives, maximising the effectiveness and sustainability of your security programme.

IT governance – an element of corporate governance aimed at improving the overall management of IT and deriving improved value from investment in information and technology – plays a vital role in aligning your cyber security and resilience activities with your wider business objectives. IT governance frameworks can help you achieve this in an effective manner, allowing you to:

- Demonstrate measurable results against broader business strategies and goals;
- Meet relevant legal and regulatory obligations;
- Assure stakeholders they can have confidence in your organisation's IT services; and
- Facilitate an increase in the return on IT investment.

See also 15.3 for a more in-depth discussion on board-level commitment and involvement, 15.4 for more on governance structure and processes and 18.3 for more information on what active support from the CEO for your security implementation project should look like.

30.1 COBIT®

COBIT – or Control Objectives for Information and Related Technology – is a framework intended to help organisations meet their business challenges in the areas of regulatory compliance, risk management and aligning IT strategy with organisational goals.

COBIT 2019, the latest iteration of the framework, is based on six principles that are essential for the effective management and governance of enterprise IT:

1. Provide stakeholder value.
2. Holistic approach.
3. Dynamic governance system.
4. Governance distinct from management.
5. Tailored to enterprise needs.
6. End-to-end governance system.

These six principles enable an organisation to build a holistic framework for the governance and management of IT that is built on seven components (previously called 'enablers'), and can be generic or 'variants of generic':

1. Processes.
2. Organisational structures.
3. Policies and procedures.
4. Information flows.
5. Culture and behaviours.
6. Skills.
7. Infrastructure.

Together, the principles and components allow an organisation to align its IT investments with its objectives to realise the value of those investments.

30.2 ISO 27014

ISO 27014 – another member of the ISO 27000 family, so designed to work well with an ISMS – gives guidance on the governance of information security, such that you can achieve strategic alignment between your information security and overall business objectives and strategy, deliver value to stakeholders and hold the governing body accountable for ensuring information security risks are adequately addressed.

Achieving these objectives requires the governing body to apply six principles:

1. Establishing organisation-wide information security.
2. Adopting a risk-based approach.
3. Setting the direction of investment decisions.
4. Ensuring conformance with internal and external requirements.
5. Fostering a security-positive environment.
6. Reviewing performance in relation to business outcomes.

However, the Standard is flexible about how, when or by whom these principles should be implemented, as the best approach will differ per organisation. That said, there are certain processes that the governing body should perform and/or enable:

- Monitoring and evaluating performance across the business;
- Giving directions in line with the organisation's security strategy and policies; and

- Bidirectional communication with stakeholders on information security activities, issues and requirements.

30.3 CRF alignment

The following table shows how our CRF, COBIT and ISO 27014 align:

Table 10: How COBIT, ISO 27014 and the CRF Align

	Baseline		CRF
	COBIT	*ISO 27014*	
Manage and protect			
Asset management			
Information security policies			
Physical and environmental security			
Identity and access control			
Malware protection			
Configuration and patch management			
Encryption			

System security			
Network and communications security			
Security competence and training			
Staff awareness training			
Comprehensive risk management programme	✓	✓	12.12
Supply chain risk management			
Identify and detect			
Threat and vulnerability intelligence			
Security monitoring			
Respond and recover			
Incident response management			
ICT continuity management			

Business continuity management			
Govern and assure			
Formal information security management programme	✓	✓	15.1
Continual improvement process	✓		15.2
Board-level commitment and involvement	✓	✓	15.3
Governance structure and processes	✓	✓	15.4
Internal audit			
External certification/ validation			

Part 6: Conclusion and appendices

CHAPTER 31: CONCLUSION

If you have made it this far, then hopefully you feel like the road towards cyber security is no longer an impossible journey. There are plenty of actions you can take that do not blow a hole in your budget or require extensive technical knowledge and experience to implement, and if you want to take things further, there are a range of standards and frameworks – including our CRF – that you can use to enhance and improve your cyber security programme, at the pinnacle of which are standards that offer a pathway to independent, external certification.

To get the best out of your cyber security programme, consider resilience and recovery alongside your cyber defence measures. A successful attack is a matter of when, not if, and a tested, effective response plan helps defend against the financial and reputational damage that follows in its wake by restoring your key revenue and support streams in a timely manner.

No matter the size of your organisation, cyber security is no longer optional – it is an essential component of business success and a critical defence against the risks of the information age. The only question left is to decide when and where your journey will begin.

APPENDIX 1: IT AND INFORMATION ASSET CHECKLIST

This non-exhaustive checklist is intended to give you an idea of what assets you should check for and record in your inventory as part of your asset management process.

- **End-user equipment**
  - Desktops
  - Laptops
  - Tablets
  - Mobile phones
  - Printers/copiers/scanners
  - Personal digital assistants (PDAs)
  - Smartwatches
- **Networking equipment**
  - Gateways
  - Routers
  - Modems
  - WAPs
  - Network bridges
  - Switches
- **Servers**
  - Email servers
  - Database servers
  - File servers
  - Web servers
  - Application servers

- **Software**
  - Application software
  - System software
  - Driver software
- **Processes**
  - Business-critical processes
  - Contractually or legally required processes
  - Processes involving personal data
- **Personnel**
  - Decision makers/management
  - Operation/maintenance staff
  - Developers
  - Users
  - Specific teams (HR, finance, marketing, sales, etc.)
- **Personal data (digital and hard copy)**
  - HR/employee data
  - Customer data (including prospects)
  - Contractor data
  - Supplier/partner data
  - Archived PII
- **Intellectual capital**
  - Employees' knowledge and skills
  - Patents, copyrights and trademarks
  - Franchises
  - Customer, supplier and partner relationships
  - Organisational reputation
- **External information systems**
  - Cloud infrastructure
  - BYOD devices

APPENDIX 2: TEMPLATE OUTLINE PROJECT PLAN

	Current state (Maturity level 1, 2, 3 or 4)	Ideal target state (Maturity level 1, 2, 3 or 4)	Process owner	Actions to take	Resources available and other relevant comments	Target date
Manage and protect						
Asset management						
Information security policies						
Physical and environmental security						
Identity and access control						
Malware protection						
Configuration and patch management						
Encryption						
System security						

	Current state	Ideal target state	Process owner	Actions to take	Resources available and other relevant comments	Target date
	(Maturity level 1, 2, 3 or 4)					
Network and communications security						
Security competence and training						
Staff awareness training						
Comprehensive risk management programme						
Supply chain risk management						
Identify and detect						
Threat and vulnerability intelligence						
Security monitoring						
Respond and recover						

	Current state	Ideal target state	Process owner	Actions to take	Resources available and other relevant comments	Target date
	(Maturity level 1, 2, 3 or 4)					
Incident response management						
ICT continuity management						
Business continuity management						
Govern and assure						
Formal information security management programme						
Continual improvement process						
Board-level commitment and involvement						
Governance structure and processes						
Internal audit						

Appendix 2: Template outline project plan

	Current state	Ideal target state	Process owner	Actions to take	Resources available and other relevant comments	Target date
	(Maturity level 1, 2, 3 or 4)					
External certification/ validation						
Overall						

APPENDIX 3: GLOSSARY OF ACRONYMS AND ABBREVIATIONS

2FA	Two-factor authentication
AD	Active Directory
BCM	Business continuity management
BCMS	Business continuity management system
BEC	Business email compromise
BIA	Business impact analysis
BYOD	Bring your own device
CPRA	California Privacy Rights Act
CIA	Confidentiality, integrity and availability
CISA	US Cybersecurity and Infrastructure Security Agency
CISO	Chief information security officer
COBIT®	Control Objectives for Information and Related Technology
CRF	IT Governance Cyber Resilience Framework
CSF	NIST Cybersecurity Framework
CVE®	Common Vulnerabilities and Exposures
CVSS	Common Vulnerability Scoring System
DDoS	Distributed denial of service
DES	Data Encryption Standard
DMZ	Demilitarised zone
DoS	Denial of service
DPA	Data Protection Act
DPO	Data protection officer
GDPR	EU General Data Protection Regulation
IAAA	Identification, authentication, authorisation and accountability
ICO	UK Information Commissioner's Office

ICT	Information and communications technology
IDS	Intrusion detection system
IoT	Internet of Things
ISMS	Information security management system
ISO	International Organization for Standardization
ITSM	IT service management
KVM	Keyboard, video, mouse
MFA	Multifactor authentication
MITM	Man in the middle
NCSC	UK National Cyber Security Centre
NDA	Non-disclosure agreement
NIS Directive	EU Directive on security of network and information systems
NIS Regulations	UK Network and Information Systems Regulations 2018
NSA	US National Security Agency
NVD	NIST National Vulnerability Database
OES	Operators of essential services
OTP	One-time passcode
OWASP	Open Web Application Security Project
PCI DSS	Payment Card Industry Data Security Standard
PDA	Personal digital assistant
PDCA	Plan-Do-Check-Act
PII	Personally identifiable information
PIMS	Privacy information management system
PKI	Public key infrastructure
PoLP	Principle of least privilege
POS	Point of sale
QMS	Quality management system

RACI	Responsible, accountable, consulted and informed
RPO	Recovery point objective
SAQ	Self-assessment questionnaire
SIEM	Security information and event management
SLA	Service level agreement
SMB	Windows Server Message Block
SoA	Statement of Applicability
SSO	Single sign-on
VLAN	Virtual local area network
VPN	Virtual private network
WAP	Wireless access point
XSS	Cross-site scripting

GRC INTERNATIONAL GROUP RESOURCES

ITGP is part of GRC International Group, which offers a comprehensive range of complementary products and services to help organisations meet their objectives.

GRC International Group is at the forefront of helping organisations globally address cyber security challenges. Our international websites are one-stop shops, providing information, advice, guidance, books, tools, training and consultancy.

For more information on cyber security and our compliance solutions, visit:

UK: *www.itgovernance.co.uk*

Europe: *www.itgovernance.eu*

Americas: *www.itgovernanceusa.com*

Asia-Pacific: *www.itgovernance.asia*

Publishing services

With books and tools covering all IT governance, risk and compliance frameworks, we are the publisher of choice for authors and distributors alike, producing unique and practical publications of the highest quality, in the latest formats available, which readers will find invaluable.

For more information about ITGP, please visit *www.itgovernancepublishing.co.uk*. Other titles published that may be of interest include:

- *The Psychology of Information Security – Resolving conflicts between security compliance and human behaviour* by Leron Zinatullin, *www.itgovernancepublishing.co.uk/product/the-psychology-of-information-security*

- *Information Security Risk Management for ISO 27001/ISO 27002, third edition* by Alan Calder and Steve G Watkins, *www.itgovernancepublishing.co.uk/product/information-security-risk-management-for-iso-27001-iso-27002-third-edition*
- *Securing Cloud Services – A pragmatic guide, second edition* by Lee Newcombe, *www.itgovernancepublishing.co.uk/product/securing-cloud-services-a-pragmatic-guide*

We also offer a range of toolkits that provide organisations with comprehensive and customisable documents to help create the specific documentation required to properly implement management systems or standards. Designed and developed by expert practitioners and based on the latest best practice, ITGP toolkits can save months of work for organisations trying to comply with a given standard.

Used by thousands of organisations worldwide, our bestselling toolkits provide you with all the templates, worksheets and policies required to ensure that you work towards and sustain being a cyber-secure and resilient organisation.

Our bestselling cyber/information security toolkits include:

- Cyber Essentials, *www.itgovernance.co.uk/shop/product/cyber-essentials-toolkit*

- ISO 27001, *www.itgovernance.co.uk/shop/product/iso-27001-toolkit*
- Cloud Security – ISO 27017 & ISO 27018, *www.itgovernance.co.uk/shop/product/cloud-security-toolkit-iso-27017-iso-27018*

Please visit *www.itgovernance.co.uk/shop/category/itgp-toolkits* to see our full range of toolkits.

Books and tools published by ITGP are available from all business booksellers and the following websites:

- *www.itgovernance.eu*
- *www.itgovernance.co.uk*
- *www.itgovernancepublishing.co.uk*
- *www.itgovernanceusa.com*
- *www.itgovernance.asia*

GRC International Group cyber security services

Some of our most popular cyber security services are listed below. For our full range of cyber security solutions, visit *www.itgovernance.co.uk/cyber-security-solutions*.

The IT Governance Cyber Resilience Framework (CRF)

For more information about the IT Governance CRF, and how you can put into practice the steps to cyber resilience discussed in this book, visit *www.itgovernance.co.uk/cyber-resilience*.

The Cyber Essentials scheme

Cyber Essentials is designed to help organisations of any size demonstrate their commitment to cyber security – while keeping the approach simple, and the costs low.

The scheme's certification process is managed by the IASME Consortium (IASME), which licenses certification bodies to carry out Cyber Essentials and Cyber Essentials Plus certifications.

For more information, visit *www.itgovernance.co.uk/cyber-essentials-scheme*.

Cyber Security as a Service (CSaaS)

With CSaaS, you can protect your organisation against cyber risks quickly, easily and cost effectively – all with one simple and affordable subscription service.

Your organisation will receive unlimited access to the Cyber Security Advice Service, vulnerability scans, assessments, staff training, guidance for process improvements and expert support.

For more information, visit *www.itgovernance.co.uk/cyber-security-as-a-service*.

Cyber security training and staff awareness

GRC International Group is a leading global provider of cyber security training courses.

Learn about cyber security, earn new qualifications and gain in-demand skills with expert-led cyber security training courses.

All courses are available in classroom, instructor-led Live Online and self-paced online formats, and offer successful participants ISO 17024-certificated qualifications from IBITGQ.

Instructor-led and self-paced online courses include:

- Cyber Security for Executive Management, *www.itgovernance.co.uk/shop/product/cyber-security-for-executive-management-instructor-led-online-training-course*
- Cyber Security for IT Support, *www.itgovernance.co.uk/shop/product/cyber-security-for-it-support-self-paced-online-training-course*
- Certified Cyber Security Foundation Training Course, *www.itgovernance.co.uk/shop/product/certified-cyber-security-foundation-training-course*

E-learning courses

Educate your staff on the key principles of cyber security with our simple-to-use, interactive, modular e-learning programme. Multi-user licences, customisation and hosting options are available.

Popular courses include:

- Cyber Security for Remote Workers Staff Awareness, *www.itgovernance.co.uk/shop/product/cyber-security-for-remote-workers-staff-awareness-e-learning-course*
- Phishing Staff Awareness Training Programme, *www.itgovernance.co.uk/shop/product/phishing-staff-awareness-training-programme*

- Information Security & ISO 27001 Staff Awareness, *www.itgovernance.co.uk/shop/product/information-security-iso27001-staff-awareness-e-learning-course*

To learn more about our cyber security training courses and to book, visit:

UK: *www.itgovernance.co.uk/cybersecurity-training*

Europe: *www.itgovernance.eu/en-ie/cyber-security-training-courses-ie*

Americas: *www.itgovernanceusa.com/shop/category/cybersecurity-training-courses*

IT Governance training centre

GRC International Group is committed to upholding the highest standards in health and hygiene, with safety a priority. That's why our purpose-built training centre in Ely, Cambridgeshire has been verified under the NQA COVID SECURE Guideline Verification Scheme, designed with comfort, convenience, health and safety in mind.

This state-of-the-art, world-class venue seamlessly brings physical and virtual audiences into one live, collaborative experience, giving you the flexibility of attending either in person, or online without losing the benefits of classroom learning.

For more information, visit *www.itgovernance.co.uk/ely-training-centre*.

Professional services and consultancy

As a compliance specialist, IT Governance has been helping organisations implement data protection programmes for more than ten years. Our specialist consultancy team has comprehensive data protection expertise and can support your cyber security projects from start to finish. We offer a wide range of services to help you meet your compliance objectives, including support with:

- Cyber security audit
- Cyber security health check
- Penetration testing
- SOC 2 audit
- Implementing an ISO 27001-compliant information security management system (ISMS)
- Data flow audit
- Establishing a personal information management system (PIMS)
- DPO as a service
- GDPR gap analysis
- Data protection impact assessment (DPIA)
- Incident management and breach reporting

For more information, visit:

UK: *www.itgovernance.co.uk/cyber-security-consultancy-services*

Europe: *www.itgovernance.eu/en-ie/cyber-security-consultancy-services-ie*

Americas: *www.itgovernanceusa.com/cybersecurity-consultancy-services*

Asia-Pacific: *www.itgovernance.asia/cyber-security-consultancy-services*

Newsletter

Subscribe to our newsletter to stay up to date with the latest developments across the whole spectrum of IT governance, including data protection and the GDPR, risk management, information security, ITIL® and IT service management, project governance, compliance, and so much more.

Simply visit our subscription centre and select your preferences:

UK: *www.itgovernance.co.uk/weekly-round-up*

Europe: *www.itgovernance.eu/en-ie/daily-sentinel-ie*

Americas: *www.itgovernanceusa.com/weekly-round-up*

Asia-Pacific: *www.itgovernance.asia/daily-sentinel*